BIG-HOOK CROCHET™

Edited by Carol Alexander

HOUSE of
WHITE
BIRCHES

PUBLISHERS
SINCE 1947

BIG-HOOK CROCHET

Copyright © 2007 House of White Birches, Berne, Indiana 46711

EDITOR Carol Alexander
ART DIRECTOR Brad Snow
PUBLISHING SERVICES MANAGER Brenda Gallmeyer

ASSOCIATE EDITOR Lisa M. Fosnaugh
ASSISTANT ART DIRECTOR Nick Pierce
COPY SUPERVISOR Michelle Beck
COPY EDITORS Beverly Richardson, Judy Weatherford
TECHNICAL EDITOR Agnes Russell

GRAPHIC ARTS SUPERVISOR Ronda Bechinski
GRAPHIC ARTISTS Jessi Butler, Minette Collins Smith
PRODUCTION ASSISTANTS Cheryl Kempf, Marj Morgan

PHOTOGRAPHY Tammy Christian, Don Clark, Matthew Owen, Jackie Schaffel
PHOTO STYLIST Tammy Nussbaum, Tammy Smith

CHIEF EXECUTIVE OFFICER David McKee
MARKETING DIRECTOR Dan Fink
Printed in China
First Printing 2007

Library of Congress Control Number: 2006920158

Hardcover ISBN: 978-1-59217-123-1
Softcover ISBN: 978-1-59217-124-8

1 2 3 4 5 6 7 8 9

A NOTE FROM THE EDITOR

With busy schedules and fast-paced lives that often keep leisure stitching time at a premium, many crocheters enjoy the easy stitching and quick results with projects that use bulky weight yarns and large size hooks.

We asked some of our top designers to create an enticing array of fun and easy fashions, accessories and home accents using all types of wonderful yarn, from the more traditional, smooth fibers to the latest high-fashion blends.

Each chapter of *Big-Hook Crochet* features projects stitched with a specific larger size hook from sizes K through P. With our tempting variety of hook-pleasing patterns designed with interesting techniques, creative stitches and tantalizing yarns, you may find it difficult to decide which project to make first!

You'll find a fabulous collection of stylish garments and trendy accessories to punch up your wardrobe for any season of the year. To dress up your decor, we've got you covered with an enticing selection of chic home accents including a variety of colorful throws, rugs and pillows.

Whatever your skill level, personal tastes or crochet preferences, you're sure to find a host of enjoyable, must-make designs in *Big-Hook Crochet* that can be easily made in whatever stitching time you have available. For these projects, big yarns and big hooks mean beautiful!

Carol Alexander

COLORFUL K-PERS

L-EGANT ACCENTS

M-BELLISH THIS!

ALWAYS N-STYLE

P-HOOK PIZZAZZ!

SIMPLY SPECTAC-Q-LAR

COLORFUL
K-PERS

Add a little dazzle to your life with colorful, creative
fashion and home pieces, all crocheted with a
size K hook. Eye-catching designs take center
stage with something to please each and every
fashionista's taste and personal sense of style!

BEADED DENIM SHRUG

Trendy fashion yarn adorns the sleeves of this eye-catching shrug, while metallic-look beads add a little extra flair. The lush suede yarn is warm and inviting, even on a chilly day.

INTERMEDIATE

5 BULKY

Finished Sizes

Instructions given fit X-small 28–30-inch bust, [small 32–34-inch bust, medium 36–38-inch bust, large 40–42-inch bust] are in brackets

Finished Garment Measurements

Finished bust measurements of shrug: 32 [36, 40, 44] inches

Gauge

2 sc = 1 inch; 5 rows = 2 inches

Pattern Notes

Weave in loose ends as work progresses.
Join rounds with a slip stitch unless otherwise stated.
Use denim unless otherwise stated.

Materials

- Lion Brand Suede bulky (chunky) weight yarn (3 oz/122 yds/85g per skein):
  3 skeins #110 denim
- Moda Dea Now bulky (chunky) weight yarn (1¾ oz/47 yds/50g per skein):
  1 skein #9832 blue bayou
- Size K/10½/6.5mm crochet hook or size needed to obtain gauge
- Tapestry needle
- 11 [12, 13, 14] each silver and blue pony beads

Back

Row 1: Beg at top, with denim, ch 33 [37, 41, 45] sc in 2nd ch from hook, sc in each rem ch across, turn. *(32 [36, 40, 44] sc)*

Rows 2–18 [2–20, 2–22, 2–24]: Ch 1, sc in each st across, turn. At the end of last rep, fasten off.

Front Panel

Make 2.

Row 1: Beg at top, ch 12 [14, 16, 18] sc in 2nd ch from hook, sc in each rem ch across, turn. *(11 [13, 15, 17] sc)*

Rows 2–8: Ch 1, sc in each st across, turn.

Row 9: Ch 1, sl st in each of first 2 sts, ch 1, sc in same st as last sl st, sc in each st across, turn. *(10 [12, 14, 16] sc)*

Row 10: Ch 1, sc in each st across, leaving last st un-worked, turn. *(9 [11, 13, 15] sc)*

Rows 11–18 [11–20, 11–22, 11–24]: Rep rows 9 and 10. At end of last rep, fasten off. *(1 sc)*
 Matching starting chs of Back with 1 Front Panel, beg at outside edge, sew tog across first 9 [11, 13, 15] sts. Rep with rem Front Panel on other side of Back.

Sleeve

Rnd 1: Working in ends of rows on outside edges of

CONTINUED ON PAGE 32

TROPICAL COLORS PURSE

As colorful as the sunset at a beach paradise, the bold coloring and random chain-stitch pattern of this bag give it dramatic, eye-catching style. Dramatic bamboo handles add flair!

INTERMEDIATE

Finished Size
10 inches tall x 11 inches wide, excluding Handles

5
BULKY

4
MEDIUM

Materials
- Moda Dea Ticker Tape bulky (chunky) weight (3¾ oz/67 yds/50g per ball):
    4 balls #9815 tropical *(CC)*
- Lion Brand Cotton Ease medium (worsted) weight yarn (3½ oz/207 yds/100g per skein):
    1 skein #157 sunflower *(MC)*
- Size K/10½/6.5mm crochet hook or size needed to obtain gauge
- Tapestry needle
- 5 x 8-inch oval bamboo handle: 2
- Stitch marker

Gauge
With CC, 14 sc = 4 inches; 15 rows = 4 inches

Pattern Notes
Weave in loose ends as work progresses.
Join rounds with a slip stitch unless otherwise stated.

Purse is crocheted with a double strand of MC and a single strand of CC.

Purse

Foundation rnd: With CC, ch 24 loosely, 3 sc in 2nd ch from hook, sc in each of next 21 ch, 3 sc in last ch, working on opposite side of foundation ch, sc in each of next 21 ch, join in beg sc. *(48 sc)*

Rnd 1: Ch 1, sc in same sc as beg ch-1, 3 sc in next sc, sc in each of next 23 sc, 3 sc in next sc, sc in each of next 22 sc, join in beg sc. *(52 sc)*

Rnd 2: Ch 1, sc in same sc as beg ch-1, sc in next sc, 3 sc in next sc, sc in each of next 25 sc, 3 sc in next sc, sc in each of next 23 sc, join in beg sc. *(25 sc)*

Rnd 3: Ch 1, sc in same sc as beg ch-1, [sc in next sc, 2 sc in next sc] twice, sc in each of next 25 sc, 2 sc in next sc, sc in next sc, 2 sc in next sc, sc in each of next 23 sc, join in beg sc. *(60 sc)*

Rnd 4: Ch 1, sc in same sc as beg ch-1, sc in each of next 3 sc, 2 sc in next sc, sc in each of next 29 sc, 2 sc in next sc, sc in each of next 25 sc, join in beg sc. *(62 sc)*

Rnd 5: Ch 1, sc in same st as beg ch-1, [sc in each of next 2 sc, 2 sc in next sc] twice, sc in each of next 27 sc, 2 sc in next sc, sc in each of next 2 sc, 2 sc in next sc, sc in each of next 24 sc, join in beg sc. *(66 sc)*

Rnd 6: Ch 1, sc in same sc as beg ch-1, sc in each of next 2 sc, 2 sc in next sc, sc in each of next 4 sc, 2 sc in next sc, sc in each of next 27 sc, 2 sc in next sc, sc in each of next 4 sc, 2 sc in next sc, sc in each of next 24 sc, join in beg sc. *(70 sc)*

Rnd 7: Ch 1, sc in same sc as beg ch-1, sc in each of next 3 sc, 2 sc in next sc, sc in each of next 4 sc, 2 sc in next sc, sc in each of next 29 sc, 2 sc in next sc, sc in each of next 4 sc, 2 sc in next sc, sc in each of next 25 sc, join in beg sc. *(74 sc)*

Rnd 8: Ch 1, sc in same sc as beg ch-1, [sc in each of next 4 sc, 2 sc in next sc] twice, sc in each of next 31 sc, 2 sc in next sc, sc in each of next 4 sc, 2 sc in next sc, sc in each of next 26 sc, join in beg sc. *(78 sc)*

Rnd 9: Ch 1, sc in same sc as beg ch-1, sc in each of next 5 sc, 2 sc in next sc, sc in each of next 4 sc, 2 sc in next sc, sc in each of next 33 sc, 2 sc in next sc, sc in each of next 4 sc, 2 sc in next sc, sc in each of next 27 sc, join in beg sc. *(82 sc)*

Rnd 10: Ch 1, sc in same sc as beg ch-1, sc in each of next 6 sc, 2 sc in next sc, sc in each of next 4 sc, 2 sc in next sc, sc in each of next 35 sc, 2 sc in next sc, sc in each of next 4 sc, 2 sc in next sc, sc in each of next 28 sc, join in beg sc. *(86 sc)*

Rnd 11: Ch 1, sc in same sc as beg ch-1, sc in each of next 7 sc, 2 sc in next sc, sc in each of next 4 sc, 2 sc in next sc, sc in each of next 37 sc, 2 sc in next sc, sc in each of next 4 sc, 2 sc in next sc, sc in each of next 29 sc, join in beg sc. *(90 sc)*

Rnd 12: Ch 1, sc in each sc around, join in beg sc.

Rnds 13–15: Rep rnd 12. At the end of rnd 15, **change color** *(see Stitch Guide)* to 2 strands MC.

Rnd 16: Ch 1, **fpsc** *(see Stitch Guide)* around post of each sc around, join in beg sc. *(90 fpsc)*

Rnd 17: Ch 1, (sc, ch 1, sc) in same st as beg ch-1, sk next 2 st, [(sc, ch 1, sc) in next st, sk next 2 sts] around, join in beg sc, turn. *(30 ch-1 sps)*

Rnd 18: Ch 1, (sc, ch 1, sc) in each ch-1 sp around, join in beg sc, turn.

Rnds 19–24: Rep rnd 18.

Rnd 25: Ch 1, [sc in next ch-1 sp, sc in sp between next 2 sc] 30 times, join in beg sc, turn. *(60 sc)*

Rnd 26: Ch 1, sc in each sc around, join in beg sc, turn.

Rnd 27 (RS): Ch 1, sc in same sc as beg ch-1, sc in each of next 2 sc, sk next sc, [sc in each of next 3 sc, sk next sc] 14 times, join in beg sc, change color to CC. *(45 sc)*

Rnd 28: Ch 1, sc in each sc around, join in beg sc.

Rnd 29: Ch 1, sc in same st as beg ch-1, [**fpdc** *(see Stitch Guide)* around sc directly below in rnd 27, sk sc directly behind fpdc, sc in next sc of rnd 28] around, join in beg sc.

Rnds 30–33: Ch 1, sc in same sc as beg ch-1, [fpdc around fpdc directly below, sc in next sc] around, join in beg sc, turn.

First Top Shaping

Row 34 (WS): Ch 1, sc in same sc as beg ch-1, sc in each of next 20 sts, turn. (21 sc)

Row 35 (RS): Ch 1, sc in same sc as beg ch-1, [fpdc

CONTINUED ON PAGE 32

HAND-PAINT MEDLEY

Rich and luxurious, the beauty of hand-painted wool
is showcased in this quick and easy hat and scarf duo.
Not only is this set fashionable, it's also warm!

EASY

MEDIUM

Finished Size
Hats: One size fits most
Scarf: 5½ x 38 inches,
   excluding Fringe

Gauge
8 dc = 2¼ inches; 5 dc rows = 2¾ inches

Pattern Notes
Weave in loose ends as work progresses.
Join rounds with a slip stitch unless otherwise stated.

Special Stitch
Loop stitch (lp st): Insert hook in next st, wrap yarn
around finger of left hand, insert hook into lp and
draw yarn through st, yo, draw through 2 lps on hook,
sl long lp off finger.

Materials
- Medium (worsted) weight
  hand-painted wool or
  wool-blend yarn:
     8 oz/425 yds/226g
        each for Hat and
        Scarf
- Size K/10½/6.5mm crochet
  hook or size needed to
  obtain gauge
- Tapestry needle

Hat
Rnd 1: Ch 4, sl st to join in first ch to form a ring, ch 2,
15 dc in ring, join in 2nd ch of beg ch-2, turn. *(16 dc)*
Rnd 2: Ch 2, dc in same st as beg ch-2, 2 dc in each st
around, join in 2nd ch of beg ch-2, turn. *(32 dc)*
Rnd 3: Rep rnd 2. *(64 dc)*
Rnd 4: Ch 2, **fpdc** *(see Stitch Guide)* around each
of next 3 sts, **bpdc** *(see Stitch Guide)* around each
of next 4sts, [fpdc around each of next 4 sts, bpdc
around each of next 4 sts] around, join in 2nd ch of
beg ch-2, turn.
Rnd 5: Ch 2, bpdc around each of next 3 sts, *fpdc
around each of next 4 sts**, bpdc around each of
next 4 sts, rep from * around, ending last rep at **,
join in 2nd ch of beg ch-2.
Rnds 6-15: Rep rnds 4 and 5 alternately. *(64 dc)*
Rnd 16: Ch 1, sc in each st around, join in beg sc. *(64 sc)*
Rnd 17: Ch 1, **lp st** *(see Special Stitch)* in each st
around, join in beg lp st.
Rnds 18–21: Rep rnds 16 and 17.
Rnd 22: Rep rnd 16, fasten off.

Scarf
Row 1: Ch 22, dc in 4th ch from hook, dc in each rem
ch across, turn. *(20 dc)*
Row 2: Ch 2, fpdc around each of next 3 sts, [bpdc

around each of next 4 sts, fpdc around each of next 4 sts] twice, turn.

Rows 3–80: Rep row 2.

Row 81: Ch 1, sc in first st, [ch 20, sc in next st] across, fasten off.

Row 82: Attach yarn in opposite side of foundation ch, ch 1, sc in same st as beg ch-1, [ch 20, sc in next st] across, fasten off. ✤

SHORTIE SWEATER

The bold vibrant colors of autumn have never looked so good! Wear this cropped sweater with your favorite jeans or cozy corduroys for a casually trendy look.

INTERMEDIATE

FINE

Finished Size
One size fits bust up to 38"

Gauge
3 shells = 4 inches; 6 rows = 4 inches

Pattern Notes
Weave in loose ends as work progresses.
Join rounds with a slip stitch unless otherwise stated.
Work with 2 strands held together unless otherwise stated.
Sweater is crocheted from wrist edge of right sleeve, ending with wrist edge of left sleeve.

Special Stitch
Shell: (3 dc, ch 3, 1 dc) in indicated st or sp.

Materials
- Red Heart Luster Sheen fine (sport) weight yarn (4 oz/335 yds/113g per skein):
  5 skeins #932 autumn
- Size K/10½/6.5mm crochet hook or size needed to obtain gauge
- Tapestry needle
- Safety pin

Right Sleeve
Row 1: Holding 2 strands of yarn tog, ch 55, **shell** *(see Special Stitch)* in 5th ch from hook, sk next 4 chs, [shell in next ch, sk next 4 chs] 9 times, dc in last ch, turn. *(10 shells)*

Row 2: Ch 3 *(counts as first dc)*, [shell in ch-3 sp of next shell] 10 times, dc in last st, turn. *(10 shells)*

Rows 3–12: Rep row 2.

Body
Row 13: Ch 18 *(forms the side seam)*, sc in 2nd ch from hook, sc in each of next 12 chs, shell in next st, sk 1 dc, shell in ch-3 sp of each shell across, turn. *(13 sc; 11 shells)*

Row 14: Ch 18 *(forms the other side seam)*, sc in 2nd ch from hook, sc in each of next 12 chs, shell in next st, sk 1 dc, shell in each ch-3 sp across, working in **back lp** *(see Stitch Guide)* of each st, sc in each of next 13 sts, turn. *(13 sc; 12 shells; 13 sc)*

Row 15: Ch 2 *(does not count as a st)*, hdc in back lp of each of next 13 sc, shell in ch-3 sp of each shell, hdc in back lp of each of next 13 sc, turn. *(13 hdc; 12 shells; 13 hdc)*

Rows 16–19: Ch 2, hdc in back lp of each hdc, shell in ch-3 sp of each shell, hdc in back lp of each hdc, turn.

Front & Neck Opening

Row 20: Ch 2, hdc in back lp of each hdc, shell in ch-3 sp of each of next 6 shells, dc between 6th and 7th shells, turn. *(13 hdc; 6 shells)*

Row 21: Ch 3, shell in ch-3 sp of each shell, hdc in back lp of each hdc across, turn.

Row 22: Ch 2, hdc in back lp of each hdc across, shell in ch-3 sp of each shell across, turn.

Rows 23–39: Rep rows 21 and 22, ending last rep with row 21. At the end of row 39, do not fasten off. Place a safety pin in the last st to secure while Back and Neck Opening is worked.

Back & Neck Opening

Row 20: Attach 2 strands at neck edge between 6th and 7th shell, ch 3, shell in ch-3 sp of each of next 6 shells, hdc in back lp of each hdc, turn. *(6 shells; 13 hdc)*

Row 21: Ch 2, hdc in back lp of each hdc, shell in ch-3 sp of each shell, dc in 3rd ch of ch-3, turn.

Row 22: Ch 3, shell in ch-3 sp of each shell, hdc in back lp of each hdc across, turn.

Rows 23–39: Rep rows 21 and 22, ending last rep with row 21, join back to front with a sl st into 3rd ch of beg ch-3 of row 39 of the front, fasten off.

Row 40: Remove safety pin and pick up dropped lp of Front, ch 2, hdc in back lp of each hdc, shell in ch-3 sp of each of next 6 shells, sk dc sts at shoulder area, working across Back, shell in ch-3 sp of each of next 6 shells, hdc in back lp of each hdc across, turn. *(13 hdc; 12 shells; 13 hdc)*

Rows 41–46: Ch 2, hdc in back lp of each hdc, shell in ch-3 sp of each shell, hdc in back lp of each hdc, turn.

Row 47: Ch 2, hdc in back lp of each hdc, shell in ch-3 sp of each of next 11 shells, dc in ch-3 sp of last shell, leaving rem sts unworked, turn. *(11 shells)*

Left Sleeve

Row 48: Ch 3, shell in ch-3 sp of each of next 10 shells, dc in ch-3 sp of last shell, turn. *(10 shells)*

Row 49: Ch 3, [shell in ch-3 sp of next shell] 10 times, dc in last st, turn.

Rows 50–60: Rep row 49. At the end of row 60, fasten off.

Finishing

With neck opening at the top, fold sweater in half, sew sleeve and side seam on each side of sweater. ❖

NEON STRIPES SCARF

With bright electric stripes dancing through denim strips, this bold scarf will jazz up even your most ordinary outfit. Pair it with a denim jacket and let the compliments pour in.

EASY

Finished Size

7 x 73 inches, excluding Fringe

5 BULKY

4 MEDIUM

Materials

- Lion Brand Color Waves bulky (chunky) weight yarn (3 oz/125 yds/85g per skein):
    - 4½ oz/188 yds/128g #309 blue lagoon
- Caron Simply Soft Brites medium (worsted) weight yarn (3 oz/ 157 yds/85g per skein):
    - 1 skein each #9604 watermelon, #9606 lemonade, and #9605 mango
- Size K/10½/6.5mm crochet hook or size needed to obtain gauge
- Tapestry needle

Gauge

2 rows = ⅞ inch; 5 sts = 2 inches

Pattern Notes

Weave in loose ends as work progresses.
Work with 2 strands held together when working with watermelon, lemonade and mango.

Scarf

Row 1 (RS): With blue lagoon, ch 182, sc in 2nd ch from hook, sc in each rem ch across **change color** *(see Stitch Guide)* to watermelon in last sc, turn. *(181 sc)*

Row 2: Ch 1, sc in first st, [dc in next st, sc in next st] across, change to blue lagoon in last st, turn.

Row 3: Ch 3 *(counts as first dc)*, [sc in next st, dc in next st] across, change color to lemonade in last st, turn.

Row 4: Rep row 2.

Row 5: Rep row 3, change color to mango in last st, turn.

CONTINUED ON PAGE 33

ILLUSION TOP

Designed to be cool on even the warmest day, this adorable little top, made in soft, comfy baby yarn, features the "illusion" of a coordinating tank.

EASY

Finished Sizes

Girl's sizes 4 [5, 6]

Chest: 22 [22, 23] inches

4

MEDIUM

Materials

- Red Heart Baby Teri medium (worsted) weight yarn (3 oz/192 yds/85g per skein):

    4 oz/256 yds/113g
    #9137 pink

- DMC Traditions size 10 crochet cotton (350 yds per ball):

    3 balls #5109
    variegated

- Size K/10½/6.5mm crochet hook or size needed to obtain gauge

- Tapestry needle

Gauge

With size K hook and medium weight yarn: 3 dc = 1 inch; 3 rows = 2 inches; crochet cotton, 2 shells = 4 inches, 2 rows = 1 inch

Check gauge to save time.

CONTINUED ON PAGE 33

HONEYMOON IN HAWAII WRAP

Make paradise yours no matter your locale when you wrap yourself in a bright and chunky little wrap featuring a wide satin ribbon. This piece is as soft as it is pretty.

EASY

BULKY

Finished Size

10 inches wide x 36 inches long, worn just off the shoulders

Gauge

Rows 1–3 = 1¾ inches; [dc, ch 1] 5 times = 4 inches
Check gauge to save time.

Pattern Note

Weave in loose ends as work progresses.

Wrap

Row 1: Ch 92, sc in 2nd ch from hook, sc in each rem ch across, turn. *(91 sc)*

Materials

- Moda Dea Swirl bulky (chunky) weight yarn (1¾ oz/62 yds/50g per ball): 4 balls #3962 tinker
- Size K/10½/6.5mm crochet hook or size needed to obtain gauge
- Yarn needle
- 48 inches ⅞-inch-wide yellow satin ribbon

Row 2: Ch 1, sc in each sc across, turn.

Row 3: Ch 4 *(counts as first dc, ch 1)*, sk next sc, dc in next sc, [sk next sc, ch 1, dc in next sc] across, turn. *(46 dc; 45 ch-1 sps)*

Row 4: Ch 3 (counts as first dc), dc in first ch-1 sp, [ch 7, sk next dc, ch-1 sp and next dc, sc in next ch-1 sp] across, ending with sc in last ch-1 sp, dc in 3rd ch of beg ch-4 of previous row, turn. *(22 ch sps)*

Row 5: Ch 3, dc in first sc, ch 3, sc in next ch-7 sp, [ch 7, sc in next ch-7 sp] across to last ch-7 sp, ch 3, sc in ch-3 sp, dc in 3rd ch of beg ch-3 of previous row, turn.

Row 6: Ch 3, dc in ch-3 sp, [ch 7, sc in next ch-7 sp] across, ending with ch 3, dc in 3rd ch of beg ch-3 of previous row, turn.

Rows 7–10: Rep row 6.

Row 11: Ch 3, 3 dc in ch-3 sp, [dc in next sc, 7 dc in next ch-7 sp] across, ending with dc in last sc, 3 dc in beg ch-3, turn.

Row 12: Ch 1, 2 sc in each dc across, fasten off. Weave ribbon through ch-1 sps of row 3, tie in front with a bow or use shawl pin to secure front. ❖

HAPPY COLORS JACKET & HAT

With a softness like silk, young ladies will love wearing this jacket and hat. Bright colors and velvety boucle yarn are sure to make this cheerful set a favorite!

INTERMEDIATE

5 BULKY

Finished Sizes
Jacket: 2 [4, 6, 8]
Hat: 2-4 [6-8]

Finished Garment Measurements
Jacket chest: 24 [26, 28, 30] inches
Head diameter: 20 [22] inches

Gauge
Size K hook: 2 sts = 1 inch; 4 rows = 3 inches

Pattern Notes
Weave in loose ends as work progresses.
Join rounds with a slip stitch unless otherwise stated.

Materials
- Caron Simply Soft Boucle bulky (chunky) weight yarn (3 oz/38 yds/85g per skein):
    Jacket: 5 skeins #285371 blue mint
    2 skeins each #0011 soft pink, #0009 limelight, #0013 grape and #0012 watermelon
    Hat: 2 [3] skeins #0005 blue mint
- Sizes J/10/6mm and K/101/2/6.5mm crochet hooks or size needed to obtain gauge
- Tapestry needle
- Stitch markers

Jacket is worked in 1 piece from lower Back over shoulders to lower Front.
Work over remaining tails left at ends of rows, keeping them on wrong side of work.

Special Stitch
Beginning half double crochet decrease (beg hdc dec): Ch 1, yo, insert hook in first st, yo, draw up a lp, insert hook in next st, yo, draw up a lp, yo and draw through all 4 lps on hook.

JACKET

Back
Row 1 (RS): With size K hook, and limelight, ch 31 [33, 35, 37], hdc in 3rd ch from hook, hdc in each rem ch across, **change color** *(see Stitch Guide)* to watermelon, turn. *(30 [32, 34, 36] hdc)*
Row 2: Ch 2 *(counts as first hdc)*, hdc in each st across, change color to grape, turn.
Note: *Rep row 2 in the following color sequence, shaping as in next step, beg with row 3, 1 row each limelight, watermelon, grape, blue mint and soft pink.*
Row 3: Beg hdc dec *(see Special Stitch)*, hdc in each st across to last 2 sts, **hdc dec** *(see Stitch Guide)* in next 2 sts, turn. *(28 [30, 32, 34] hdc)*

Row 4: Ch 2, hdc in each hdc across, turn.
Row 5: Rep row 4.
Rows 6–11: Rep rows 3–5. *(24 [26, 28, 30] hdc)*
Rows 12–18 [21, 25, 28]: Rep row 4.

Left Front

Note: *Work 1 row with same color as used for last stripe of Jacket Back. Reverse color sequence so that colors match when pieces are assembled.*
Row 1: Ch 2, hdc in each of next 7 [8, 8, 9] sts, turn. *(8 [9, 9, 10] hdc)*
Row 2: Ch 2, hdc in same st as beg ch-2, hdc in each st to end, turn. *(9 [10, 10, 11] hdc)*
Row 3: Ch 2, hdc in each st across to last st, 2 hdc in last st, turn. *(10 [11, 11, 12] hdc)*
[Rep rows 2 and 3] 3 [3, 4, 4] times. *(13 [14, 15, 16] hdc)*
Work even in hdc in reverse color sequence until Left Front is same length as Back to lower shaping. When Left Front and Back pieces match for shaping to beg, [inc 1 st at side edge every 3 rows] 3 times. *(16 [17, 18, 19] hdc)*
Continuing in reverse color sequence, work 2 rows even in hdc, fasten off.

Right Front

Row 1: Sk 8 [8, 10, 10] sts for center back neck, attach yarn to next st, ch 2, hdc in each of next 7 [8, 8, 9] sts, turn. *(8 [9, 9, 10] hdc)*
Row 2: Ch 2, hdc in each st across to last st, 2 hdc in last st, turn. *(9 [10, 10, 11] hdc)*
Row 3: Ch 2, hdc in same st as beg ch-2, hdc in each rem st across, turn. *(10 [11, 11, 12] hdc)*
[Rep rows 2 and 3] 3 [3, 4, 4] times. *(13 [14, 15, 16] hdc)*
Work even in hdc in reverse color sequence until

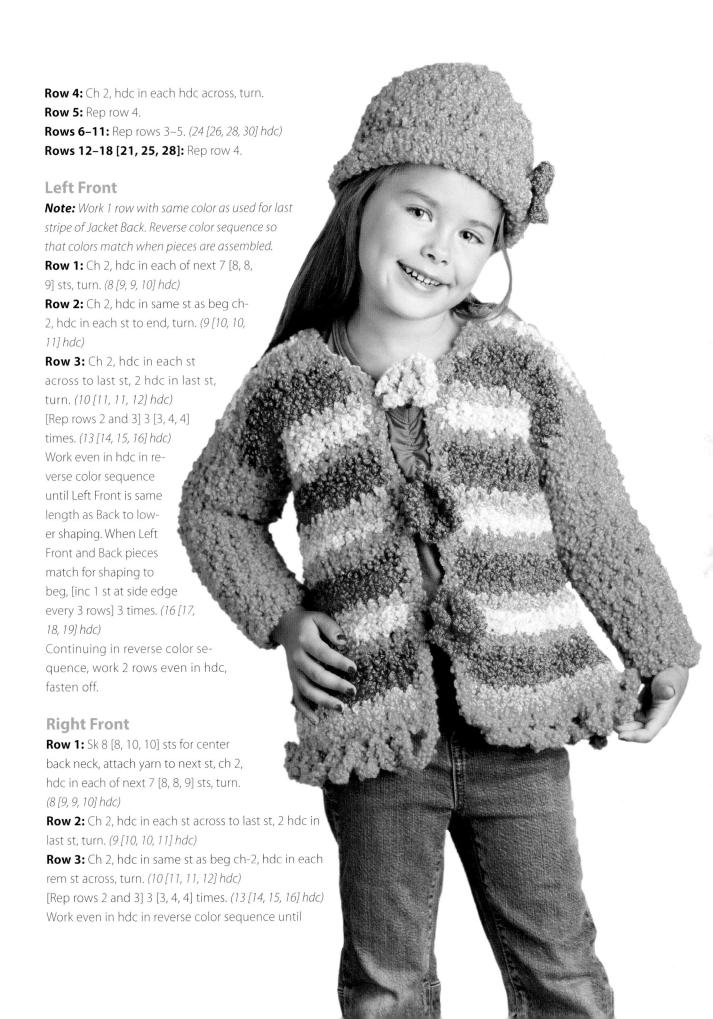

Right Front and Back pieces match for shaping to beg, [inc 1 st at side edge every 3 rows] 3 times. *(16 [17, 18, 19] hdc)*

Continuing in reverse color sequence, work 2 rows even in hdc, fasten off.

Sleeve

Make 2.

Note: *For sleeve opening, place st markers 4½ [5, 5½, 6] inches on either side of shoulder.*

Row 1 (RS): With size K hook, attach blue mint, ch 1, work 10 [11, 12, 13] sc from marker to shoulder, work another 10 [11, 12, 13] sc from shoulder to marker, turn. *(20 [22, 24, 26] hdc)*

Row 2: Ch 2, hdc in each st across, turn.

Row 3: Rep row 2.

Row 4: Beg hdc dec, hdc in each st across to last 2 st, hdc dec in last 2 sts, turn. *(18 [20, 22, 24] hdc)*

Row 5: Rep row 2.

[Rep rows 4 and 5] 3 [3, 4, 4] times. *(12 [14, 14, 16] hdc)*

Rep row 2 until Sleeve measures approximately 8½ [10½, 11½, 12½] inches in length, fasten off.

Sew side and sleeve seams in continuous seam.

Outer Edging

Rnd 1 (RS): With size J hook, attach blue mint at side seam, ch 1, sc evenly sp around entire outer edge, working 3 sc in each corner and at beg of V-neck shaping, sl st to join in beg sc, fasten off.

Row 2 (WS): Working across to bottom edge of Jacket, with size J hook, attach blue mint in first st, [ch 7, sk 1 st, sl st in next st] across, fasten off.

Flower

Make 3.

Rnd 1: With size J hook and blue mint, ch 2, 7 sc in 2nd ch from hook, sl st to join in beg sc, fasten off. *(7 sc)*

Rnd 2: Attach soft pink in any sc, [ch 3, sl st in next sc] around, fasten off. *(7 ch-3 lps)*

For 2nd flower, work rnd 2 with grape; for 3rd flower,

work rnd 2 with watermelon.

Sew flowers evenly sp to Left Front.

Button Loops

Make 3.

With size J hook, attach blue mint to right front matching position to center of flower, ch 9, sl st in same st where yarn was attached, fasten off. Button lps fit snugly around each Flower.

HAT

Crown

Rnd 1: With size K hook and blue mint, ch 2, 8 sc in 2nd ch from hook, use st marker to mark rnds, do not join. *(8 sc)*

Rnd 2: 2 sc in each sc around. *(16 sc)*

Rnd 3: [Sc in next sc, 2 sc in next sc] 8 times. *(24 sc)*

Rnd 4: [Sc in each of next 2 sc, 2 sc in next sc] 8 times. *(32 sc)*

Rnd 5: [Sc in each of next 3 sc, 2 sc in next sc] 8 times. *(40 sc)*

Rnd 6 (sizes 6–8 only): [Sc in each of next 9 sc, 2 sc in next sc] 4 times. *(44 sc)*

Rnd 7 (both sizes): Sc in each sc around.

Rep rnd 7 until Hat Crown measures 6 inches from center of crown, ending in line with st marker.

Brim

Rnd 1: [Sc in each of next 4 sc, 2 sc in next sc] 8 [8] times, sc in each of next 0 [4] sc. *(48 [56] sc)*

Rnds 2 & 3: Sc in each sc around. At the end of rnd 3, sl st in next sc, fasten off.

Flower

Rnd 1: With size J hook and blue mint, ch 2, 7 sc in 2nd ch from hook, sl st to join in beg sc, fasten off. *(7 sc)*

Rnd 2: Attach watermelon in any sc, [ch 3, sl st in next sc] around, fasten off. *(7 ch-3 lps)* Turn 2 rnds of brim upward. Sew Flower to Hat Brim. ❧

BUG RUG

Certainly much cuter than your garden variety bug, this darling mat created in bright colors will provide hours of fun for a toddler or small child.

INTERMEDIATE

6 SUPER BULKY

Finished Sizes

Head: 11 inches in diameter
Body: 27 inches in diameter

Materials

- Lion Brand Thick & Quick Chenille super bulky (super chunky) weight yarn (100 yds/99g per skein):
    - 3 skeins #130 grass green
    - 1 skein #157 lemon
- Lion Brand Boucle super bulky (super chunky) weight yarn (2½ oz/57 yds/70g per skein):
    - 4 skeins #202 lime blue
    - 1 skein #106 blueberry

Gauge

2 sc = 1 inch; 2 sc rows = 1 inch; 3 hdc = 1 inch; 2 hdc rows = 1 inch; 3 dc = 1 inch; 3 dc rows = 2 inches

- Size K/10½/6.5mm crochet hook or size needed to obtain gauge
- Tapestry needle
- Sewing needle
- Sewing needle to take ribbon
- 1-inch plastic squeakers: 2
- 35mm electronic music boxes/buttons: 2
- Fiberfill
- 10 yd reel ¼-inch-wide pink ribbon
- 10 yd reel ⅛-inch-wide light blue and hot pink
- 2-inch embroidered floral appliqué
- Baby teething rings: 10 or 11

Pattern Notes

Weave in loose ends as work progresses.
Join rounds with a slip stitch unless otherwise stated.

Body

Rnd 1 (RS): With grass green, ch 4, sl st in first ch to form a ring, ch 3 (counts as first dc), dc in ring, **change color** (see Stitch Guide) to lime blue, drop grass green to WS, dc in ring, [drop lime blue, pick up grass green, 2 dc in ring, drop grass green, pick up lime blue, dc in ring] 5 times, drop lime blue, pick up grass green, join in 3rd ch of beg ch-3, do not turn. (18 sts)

Rnd 2: Sl st in next dc, ch 3, 2 dc in same st as beg ch-3, change to lime blue, dc in next 2 sts, [change to grass green, 3 dc in next st, change to lime blue, dc in next 2 sts] 5 times, change to grass green, join in 3rd ch of beg ch-3, do not turn. (30 sts)

Rnd 3: Sl st in next dc, ch 3, 2 dc in next st, dc in next st, change to lime blue, dc in next 2 sts, [change to grass green, dc in next st, 2 dc in next st, dc in next st, change to lime blue, dc in next 2 sts] 5 times, change to grass green, sl st to join in 3rd ch of beg ch-3. (36 sts)

Rnd 4: Sl st in next dc, ch 3, dc in same st as beg ch-3, dc in next st, 2 dc in next st, dc in next st, change to lime blue, 2 dc in next st, dc in next st, [change to grass green, {2 dc in next st, dc in next st} twice,

change to lime blue, 2 dc in next st, dc in next st] 5 times, change to grass green, join in 3rd ch of beg ch-3, do not turn. *(54 sts)*

Rnd 5: Sl st in next dc, ch 3, dc in each of next 5 sts, change to lime blue, dc in each of next 3 sts, [change to grass green, dc in each of next 6 sts, change to lime blue, dc in each of next 3 sts] around, change to grass green, join in 3rd ch of beg ch-3, do not turn.

Rnd 6: Sl st in next dc, ch 3, dc in same st as beg ch-3, dc in next st, [2 dc in next st, dc in next st] twice, change to lime blue, dc in next 3 sts, *change to grass green, [2 dc in next st, dc in next st] 3 times, change to lime blue, dc in next 3 sts, rep from * around, change to grass green, join in 3rd ch of beg ch-3, do not turn. *(72 sts)*

Rnd 7: Sl st in each of next 2 sts, ch 3, dc in each of next 7 sts, change to lime blue, dc in each of next 4 sts, [change to grass green, dc in each of next 8 sts, change to lime blue, dc in next 4 sts] around, change to grass green, join in 3rd ch of beg ch-3, do not turn.

Rnd 8: Sl st in next 2 sts, ch 3, dc in next st, [2 dc in next st, dc in each of next 2 sts] twice, 2 dc in next st, *change to lime blue, dc in next 2 sts, 2 dc in next st, dc in next st, change to grass green**, [dc in next 2 st, 2 dc in next st, dc in each of next 2 sts] twice, 2 dc in next st, rep from * around, ending last rep at **, join in 3rd ch of beg ch-3, do not turn. *(102 sts)*

Rnd 9: Sl st in next st, ch 3, dc in each of next 11 sts, *change to lime blue, dc in next 5 sts, [change to grass green, dc in next 12 sts, change to lime blue, dc in next 5 sts] around, change to grass green, join in 3rd ch of beg ch-3, do not turn.

Rnd 10: Sl st in next st, ch 3, 2 dc in next st, dc in next st, [2 dc in next st, dc in next 2 sts] 3 times, *change to lime blue, 2 dc in next st, dc in next 4 sts, change to grass green**, dc in next st, 2 dc in next st, dc in next st, [2 dc in next st, dc in each of next 2 sts] 3 times, rep from * around, ending last rep at **, join in 3rd ch of beg ch-3, do not turn. *(132 sts)*

Rnd 11: Sl st in next st, ch 3, dc in each of next 15 sts, *change to lime blue, dc in next 6 sts, change to grass green**, dc in each of next 16 sts, rep from * around, ending last rep at **, join in 3rd ch of beg ch-3, do not turn.

Rnd 12: Sl st in next st, ch 3, dc in same st as beg ch-3, dc in next 3 sts, [2 dc in next st, dc in each of next 3 sts] 3 times, *change to lime blue, 2 dc in next st, dc in next 5 sts, change to grass green**, 2 dc in next st, dc in each of next 3 sts] 4 times, rep from * around, ending last rep at **, join in 3rd ch of beg ch-3, do not turn. *(162 sts)*

Rnds 13 & 14: Sl st in next st, ch 3, dc in next 19 sts, *change to lime blue, dc in each of next 7 sts, change to grass green**, dc in next 20 sts, rep from * around, ending last rep at **, join in 3rd ch of beg ch-3, do not turn.

Rnd 15: Sl st in next st, ch 3, dc in same st as beg ch-3, dc in each of next 4 sts, [2 dc in next st, dc in each of next 4 sts] 3 times, *change to lime blue, 2 dc in next st, dc in next 4 sts, 2 dc in next st, dc in next st, change to grass green**, [2 dc in next dc, dc in next 4 dc] 4 times, rep from * around, ending last rep at **, join in 3rd ch of beg ch-3, do not turn. *(198 sts)*

Rnds 16 & 17: Sl st in next st, ch 3, dc in each of next 23 sts, *change to lime blue, dc in each of next 9 sts, change to grass green**, dc in each of next 24 sts, rep from * around, ending last rep at **, join in 3rd ch of beg ch-3, do not turn. At the end of rnd 17, fasten off.

Leg

Make 4.

Row 1: With lime blue, ch 18, hdc in 2nd ch from hook, hdc in each rem ch across, turn. *(17 sts)*

Rows 2 & 3: Ch 1, hdc in each hdc across, turn.

Row 4: Ch 1, **hdc dec** *(see Stitch Guide)* in next 2 sts, hdc in each rem st across, turn. *(16 sts)*

Rows 5–13: Rep row 4. *(7 sts)*

Rows 14 & 15: Ch 1, hdc dec in next 2 sts, hdc in each st to last 2 sts, hdc dec in next 2 sts, turn. *(3 sts)* At the end of row 15, fasten off.

Teething Ring Tabs

Make 10.

Row 1: With grass green ch 2, sc in 2nd ch from hook, turn. *(1 st)*

Rows 2–10: Ch1, sc in sc, turn. At the end of row 10, fasten off.

Fold Teething Ring Tabs in half and sew 5 Tabs around 2 of the Legs, making sure to sp evenly. Insert teething rings into tabs.

Music Button Square

Row 1: With grass green, ch 7, sc in 2nd ch from hook, sc in each rem ch across, turn. *(6 sts)*

Row 2: Ch 1, sc in each sc across, turn.

Rows 3–7: Ch 1, sk first st, sc in each rem st across, turn. *(1 st)* At the end of row 7, fasten off. Sew triangle to underside of a Leg, inserting music button inside before closing.

Head

Make 2.

Rnd 1: With lemon, ch 3, sl st in first ch to form a ring, ch 1, work 8 hdc in ring, join in top of first hdc, turn. *(8 sts)*

Rnd 2: Ch 1, [2 hdc in next st, hdc in next st] around, join in top of first hdc, turn. *(12 sts)*

Rnds 3 & 4: Rep rnd 2. *(27 sts)*

Rnd 5: Ch 1, hdc in next st, [2 hdc in next st, hdc in next st] around, join in top of first hdc, turn. *(40 sts)*

Rnd 6: Ch 1, hdc in next st, [2 hdc in next st, hdc in each of next 2 sts] around, join in top of first hdc, turn. *(53 sts)*

Rnd 7: Ch 1, hdc in each hdc around, join in top of first hdc, turn.

Rnd 8: Ch 1, hdc in each of next 2 sts, [2 hdc in next st, hdc in each of next 2 sts] around, join in top of first hdc, turn. *(70 sts)*

Rnd 9: Rep rnd 7, fasten off. Sew Head sections tog stuffing with fiberfill before closing.

Hat

Rnd 1: With blueberry, ch 11, 2 sc in 2nd ch from hook, sc in each of next 8 chs, 2 sc in next ch, working on opposite side of foundation ch, sc in each of next 8 chs, join in beg sc, turn. *(20 sts)*

Rnd 2: Ch 1, 2 sc in each of next 2 sts, sc in each of next 6 sts, 2 sc in each of next 4 sts, 2 sc in each of next 2 sts, join in beg sc, turn. *(28 sts)*

Rnds 3–5: Ch 1, sc in each st around, join in beg sc, turn.

Rnd 6: Ch 1, [2 sc in next st, sc in each of next 3 sts] around, join in beg sc, turn. *(35 sts)*

Rnd 7: Ch 1, hdc in each st around, join in top of first hdc, turn.

CONTINUED ON PAGE 35

EDWARD THE SWEATER BEAR

Almost as handsome as he is cuddly, this darling bear is stylish in his very own crocheted sweater. Delight a young child or just someone young-at-heart with this special bear!

EASY

5 BULKY

Finished Size
14 inches tall

4 MEDIUM

Materials
- Lion Brand Homespun bulky (chunky) weight yarn (6 oz/185 yds/170g per skein):
  1 skein #318 sierra
  2 oz/61 yds/566 each
  #302 colonial, #307 antique, #321 Williamsburg and #372 sunshine state
- Medium (worsted) weight yarn:
  1 yd black
- Size K/10½/6.5mm crochet hook or size needed to obtain gauge
- Yarn needle
- 12mm black animal eyes: 2
- Fiberfill
- Stitch marker

Gauge
3 sc = 1 inch; 3 sc rows = 1 inch

Pattern Notes
Weave in loose ends as work progresses.
Do not join rounds with unless otherwise stated. Use stitch marker to mark rnds.

Head
Rnd 1: With sierra, ch 2, 6 sc in 2nd ch from hook. *(6 sc)*
Rnd 2: 2 sc in each st around. *(12 sc)*

Rnd 3: [Sc in next st, 2 sc in next st] around. *(18 sc)*
Rnd 4: [Sc in each of next 2 sts, 2 sc in next st] around. *(24 sc)*
Rnd 5: [Sc in each of next 3 sts, 2 sc in next st] around. *(30 sc)*
Rnd 6: [Sc in each of next 4 sts, 2 sc in next st] around. *(36 sc)*
Rnd 7: [Sc in each of next 5 sts, 2 sc in next st] around. *(42 sc)*
Rnd 8: [Sc in each of next 6 sts, 2 sc in next st] around. *(48 sc)*

Rnd 9: Sc in each st around.

Rnds 10–18: Rep rnd 9.

Rnd 19: [Sc in each of next 6 sts, **sc dec** (see Stitch Guide) in next 2 sts] around. (42 sc)

Rnd 20: [Sc in each of next 5 sts, sc dec in next 2 sts] around. (36 sc)

Rnd 21: [Sc in each of next 4 sts, sc dec in next 2 sts] around. (30 sc)

Rnd 22: [Sc in each of next 3 sts, sc dec in next 2 sts] around. (24 sc)

Rnd 23: [Sc in each of next 2 sts, sc dec in next 2 sts] around. (18 sc)

Stuff Head with fiberfill; for Eyes, wait until after rnd 28 to attach to see where the armholes are so that you can center Eyes accordingly.

Body

Rnds 24: Rep rnd 4, **change color** (see Stitch Guide) to colonial. (24 sc)

Rnds 25 & 26: Rep rnds 5 and 6. (36 sc)

Rnd 27: Rep rnd 2. (72 sc)

Rnd 28: Sc in each of next 12 sts, sk next 18 sts (armhole), sc in each of next 18 sts, sk next 18 sts (armhole), sc in next 6 sts. (36 sc)

Secure Eyes between rnds 14 and 15 with about 2 sts between Eyes.

Rnd 29: [Sc in next 5 sts, 2 sc in next st] around, change color to Williamsburg. (42 sc)

Rnd 30: [Sc in each of next 6 sts, 2 sc in next st] around, change color to antique. (48 sc)

Rnd 31: Rep rnd 9, change color to sunshine state.

Rnd 32: Rep rnd 9, change color to antique.

Rnd 33: Rep rnd 9, change color to Williamsburg.

Rnd 34: Rep rnd 9, change color to colonial.

Rnds 35–38: Rep rnd 9.

Rnd 39: Rep rnd 9, change color to sierra.

Rnds 40–43: Rep rnd 9.

Rnds 44–48: Rep rnds 19–23. (18 sc)

Rnd 49: [Sc in next st, sc dec in next 2 sts] around. (12 sc)

Rnd 50: [Sc dec in next 2 sts] around, sl st in next st, leaving a length of yarn, fasten off. (6 sc)

Stuff Body with fiberfill, sew opening closed.

Arm

Make 2.

Rnd 1: Working in sk sts of rnd 27, attach colonial with sc at underarm, sc in each of next 17 sc. (18 sc)

Rnd 2: Sc in each sc around, change color to Williamsburg.

Rnd 3: Sc in each sc around, change color to antique.

Rnd 4: Sc in each sc around, change color to sunshine state.

Rnd 5: Sc in each st around, change color to antique.

Rnd 6: Sc in each st around, change color to Williamsburg.

Rnd 7: Sc in each st around, change color to colonial.

Rnds 8–12: Sc in each st around. At the end of rnd 12, change color to sierra.

Rnds 13–15: Sc in each st around.

Stuff Arm with fiberfill and continue stuffing as needed.

Rnd 16: [Sc in next st, sc dec in next 2 sts] around. (12 sc)

Rnd 17: [Sc dec in next 2 sts] around, sl st in next st, leaving a length of yarn, fasten off. (6 sc) Sew opening closed.

Leg

Make 2.

Rnd 1: With sierra, ch 6, 3 sc in 2nd ch from hook, sc in each of next 3 chs, 6 sc in last ch, working on opposite side of foundation ch, sc in each of next 3 chs, 3 sc in same ch as beg 3 sc, join with sl st in beg sc. (18 sc)

Rnd 2: Ch 3 (counts as first dc), dc in same st as beg ch-3, 2 dc in each of next 2 sts, dc in each of next 3 sts, 2 dc in each of next 6 sts, dc in each of next 3 sts, 2 dc in each of next 3 sts, join with sl st in 3rd ch of beg ch-3. (30 dc)

Rnd 3: Ch 1, sc in same st as beg ch-1, sc in each of next 8 sts, [**dc dec** (see Stitch Guide) in next 2 sts] 6 times, sc in each of next 9 sts, do not join, use a st marker. (24 sts)

Rnd 4: Sc in each of next 9 sts, [dc dec in next 2 sts] 3 times, sc in next 9 sts. (21 sts)

Rnds 5–18: Sc in each st around.

CONTINUED ON PAGE 35

FLORAL GRANNY AFGHAN

Soft summery colors and the classic beauty of granny squares make this pretty floral afghan one that you'll love to have in any room of your home.

Finished Sizes
Afghan: 45 x 64 inches
Block: 6 inches square

Gauge
Rnds 1–3 = 3¼ inches; 9 dc of border = 3 inches

Pattern Notes
Weave in loose ends as work progresses.
Join rounds with a slip stitch unless otherwise stated.
Rnd 1 establishes right side of block.
Each block is made using 3 different colors with white. Colors will be indicated as color 1, 2 and 3.

Materials
- Red Heart TLC Essentials medium (worsted) weight yarn (6 oz/312 yds/170g per skein):
  - 6 skeins #2101 white
  - 1 skein each #2772 light country rose, #2220 butter, #2531 light plum, #2883 country blue and #2672 light thyme
- Size K/10½/6.5mm crochet hook or size needed to obtain gauge
- Tapestry needle

Special Stitches
Popcorn (pc): 5 dc in ring, draw up a lp, remove hook, insert hook in first dc of 5-dc group, pick up dropped lp and draw through st on hook.

Beginning popcorn (beg pc): Ch 3, 4 dc in ring, draw up a lp, remove hook, insert hook in top of beg ch-3, pick up dropped lp and draw through st on hook.

Block
Make 70.
Rnd 1 (RS): With color 1, ch 5, sl st to join in beg ch to form a ring, **beg pc** (see Special Stitches) in ring, ch 5, [**pc** (see Special Stitches) in ring, ch 5] 3 times, join in 3rd ch of beg ch-3 of pc, fasten off. (4 pc)

Rnd 2: Attach color 2 with sl st in top of beg pc, *ch 3, work 2 dc in next corresponding sp between pc sts into ch-5 ring of rnd 1, drawing dc up to current level of working rnd, ch 3, sl st in top of next pc, rep from * around, fasten off. (8 dc; 8 ch-3 sps)

Rnd 3: Attach white in first ch-3 sp of previous rnd, ch 3 (counts as first dc), 2 dc in same ch-3 sp, ch 1, sk next 2 dc, 3 dc in next ch-3 sp, ch 2, *3 dc in next ch-3 sp, ch 1, sk next 2 dc, 3 dc in next ch-3 sp, ch 2, rep from * around, join in 3rd ch of beg ch-3. (24 dc; 4 ch-1 sps; 4 ch-2 sps)

Rnd 4: Sl st into next ch-1 sp, ch 3, 3 dc in same ch-1

sp, sk next 3 dc, (4 dc, ch 2, 4 dc) in next ch-2 sp, *sk next 3 dc, 4 dc in next ch-1 sp, sk next 3 dc, (4 dc, ch 2, 4 dc) in next ch-2 sp, rep from * around, join in 3rd ch of beg ch-3, fasten off. *(48 dc, 4 corner ch-2 sps)*

Rnd 5: Attach color 3 with sl st in corner ch-2 sp, *(2 hdc, ch 2, 2 hdc) in corner ch-2 sp, [sk next 2 dc, 2 hdc between 2 sk dc and next dc] 5 times, sk next 2 dc, rep from * around, join in top of first hdc, fasten off. *(56 hdc; 4 corner ch-2 sps)*

Rnd 6: Attach white in corner ch-2 sp, ch 3, (dc, ch 2, 2 dc) in same corner ch-2 sp, *[sk next 2 hdc, 2 dc between 2 sk hdc and next hdc] 6 times, sk next 2 hdc**, (2 dc, ch 2, 2 dc) in next corner ch-2 sp, rep from * around, ending last rep at **, join in 3rd ch of beg ch-3, fasten off. *(64 dc; 4 corner ch-2 sps)*

Assembly

When joining Blocks, make sure that each junction of 4 blocks and all other corners are evenly secured so Afghan will not be distorted.

With RS facing, using white, sl st Blocks tog in a pattern of 7 x 10 working in **back lp** *(see Stitch Guide)* of corresponding sts on WS and matching sts from corner to corner.

Border

Rnd 1 (RS): Attach white in top right corner ch-2 sp, ch 3, (dc, ch 2, 2 dc) in same corner ch-2 sp, *dc in each dc across to next joining seam, 2 dc in joining seam, rep from * around, working (2 dc, ch 2, 2 dc) in each rem corner ch-2 sp, join in 3rd ch of beg ch-3.

Rnd 2: Ch 1, sc in each dc around, working 3 sc in each corner ch-2 sp, join in beg sc.

Rnd 3: Ch 1, sc in each of next 2 sc, (ch 3, sl st) in next sc, [sc in each of next 2 sc, (ch 3, sl st) in next sc] around, join in beg sc, fasten off. ❖

AUTUMN WOODS RUG

Keep your toes warm on a chilly morning when you step onto this luxuriously soft rug. Created in rich colors, it will look pretty in any room in your home.

INTERMEDIATE

Finished Size
24 x 33 inches, excluding Fringe

4 MEDIUM

5 BULKY

Materials
- Red Heart Super Saver medium (worsted) weight yarn (8 oz/452 yds/226g per skein):
  2 skeins #412 farmland
- Lion Brand Lion Suede bulky (chunky) weight yarn (3 oz/122 yds/85g per skein):
  3 skeins #126 coffee
  1 skein each #133 spice and #132 olive
- Size K/10½/6.5mm crochet hook or size needed to obtain gauge
- Tapestry needle

Gauge
Rows 1–3 = 2¼ inches at shell point; 6 sc across first row = 1¼ inches

Pattern Notes
Weave in loose ends as work progresses.
Join rounds with a slip stitch unless otherwise stated.
Work Rug in rows on both sides of center foundation ch as indicated.
Work with 2 strands of yarn held together throughout. Leave a 7-inch length of yarn to beg and when fastening off to tie into final fringe.

Special Stitches
Shell: 5 dc in indicated st.
Beginning half shell (beg half shell): Ch 3 (counts as first dc), 2 dc in same sc as beg ch-3.
Ending half shell: 3 dc in last sc.

First Half
Row 1 (RS): With farmland and coffee, ch 74, sc in 2nd ch from hook, sc in each rem ch across, turn. (73 sc)
Row 2: Ch 1, sc in first sc, [sk next 2 sc, **shell** (see Special Stitch) in next sc, sk next 2 sc, sc in next sc] 12 times, fasten off, turn. (12 shells; 13 sc)
Row 3: Draw up a lp of farmland and olive, **beg half shell** (see Special Stitches) in first sc, [sc in center dc of next shell, shell in next sc] 11 times, sc in center dc of next shell, **ending half shell** (see Special Stitches) in last sc, fasten off, turn. (2 half shells; 11 shells; 12 sc)
Row 4: Draw up a lp of farmland and coffee in end dc, ch 1, sc in same dc as beg ch-1, [shell in next sc, sc in center dc of next shell] 11 times, shell in next sc, sk next 2 dc, sc in next dc, fasten off, turn. (12 shells; 13 sc)

Row 5: Draw up a lp of farmland and spice, beg half shell in first sc, [sc in center dc of next shell, shell in next sc] 11 times, sc in center dc of next shell, ending half shell in last sc, turn.

Row 6: Ch 1, sc in first dc, [shell in next sc, sc in center dc of next shell] 11 times, shell in next sc, sk next 2 dc, sc in next dc, fasten off, turn.

Continuing in pat st for rows 3 and 4 and fastening off when necessary or working ch 1 or ch 3 to beg next row and alternating RS and WS, work the following.

Rows 7–9: Work 3 rows in farmland and coffee.

Row 10: Work 1 row with farmland and olive.

Row 11: Work 1 row with farmland and coffee.

Rows 12 & 13: Work 2 rows in farmland and spice.

Rows 14–16: Work 3 rows in farmland and coffee.

Row 17: Continuing in farmland and coffee, sc in first sc, *ch 2, sk 2 dc, (sc, ch 2, sc) in next dc, ch 2, sk 2 dc, sc in next sc, rep from * across, fasten off.

2nd Half

Row 1 (RS): Working on opposite side of foundation ch of First Half, draw up a lp of farmland and coffee, ch 1, sc in same ch as beg ch-1, sc in each rem ch across, turn. *(73 sc)*

Rows 2–17: Rep rows 2–17 of First Half.

Fringe

Add lengths to end of each sc row and twice on end of each dc row. Cut 14-inch lengths of yarn to match ends of rows. Add 2 lengths *(1 medium weight and 1 suede)* where there are no tails and 1 of medium weight only where there are tails. Fold lengths in half and tie in an overhand knot tying in tails. Trim to desired length. ✤

BEADED DENIM SHRUG CONTINUED FROM PAGE 8

Front Panel and Back, join with sc in end of row 18 [20, 22, 24] on Front Panel, sc in each row around, join with sl st in beg sc, turn. *(36 [40, 44, 48] sc)*

Rnds 2–5: Ch 1, sc in each st around, join with sl st in beg sc, turn.

Rnd 6: Ch 1, sc in each of first 7 [8, 9, 10] sts, **sc dec** *(see Stitch Guide)* in next 2 sts, *sc in each of next 7 [8, 9, 10] sts, sc dec in next 2 sts, rep from * around, join with sl st in beg sc, turn. *(32 [36, 40, 44] sc)*

Rnds 7–11: Ch 1, sc in each st around, join with sl st in beg sc, turn.

Rnd 12: Ch 1, *sc in each of next 6 [7, 8, 9] sts, sc dec in next 2 sts, rep from * around, join with sl st in beg sc, turn. *(28 [32, 36, 40] sc)*

Rnds 13–17: Ch 1, sc in each st around, join with sl st in beg sc, turn.

Rnd 18: Ch 1, *sc in each of next 5 [6, 7, 8] sts, sc dec in next 2 sts, rep from * around, join with sl st in beg sc, turn. *(24 [28, 32, 36] sc)*

Rnds 19–23: Ch 1, sc in each st around, join with sl st in beg sc, turn.

Rnd 24: Ch 1, *sc in each of next 4 [5, 6, 7] sts, sc dec in next 2 sts, rep from * around, join with sl st in beg sc, turn. *(20 [24, 28, 32] sc)*

X-Small & Small Sizes Only

Rnds 25–39: Ch 1, sc in each st around, join with sl st in beg sc, turn. At the end of last rep, fasten off.

Medium & Large Sizes Only

Rnd 25: Ch 1, *sc in each of next [5, 6] sts, sc dec in next 2 sts, rep from * around, join with sl st in beg sc, turn. *([24, 28] sc)*

Medium Size Only

Rnds 26–39: Ch 1, sc in each st around, join with sl st in beg sc, turn. At the end of last rnd, fasten off.

Large Size Only

Rnd 26: Ch 1, [sc in each of next 5 sts, sc dec in next 2 sts] around, join with sl st in beg sc, turn. *(24 sc)*

Rnds 27–39: Ch 1, sc in each st around, join with sl st in beg sc, turn. At end of last rnd, fasten off.

Rep sleeve on outside edge of rem Front Panel and Back. Sew underarm Sleeve seams.

Sleeve Trim

Working around end of Sleeve, attach blue bayou with sl st in seam, ch 3 *(counts as first dc)*, 4 dc in same st, 5 dc in each st around, join with sl st in 3rd ch of beg ch-3, fasten off.

Rep Sleeve Trim on rem Sleeve.

Front Shaping

Rnd 1: Thread beads onto denim alternating colors, working in ends of rows and in sts around Front Panels, attach denim with sc in first st at Bottom Back, evenly sp work 89 [97, 105, 113] sc around, join with sl st in beg sc, turn. *(90 [98, 106, 114] sc)*

Rnd 2: Ch 1, sc in first st, draw up a bead, ch 1, sk next st, [sc in next st, draw up a bead, ch 1, sk next st] 10 [11, 12, 13] times, sc in each st around to next Front Panel, [draw up a bead, ch 1, sk next st, sc in next st] 11 [12, 13, 14] times, sc in each st across, join with sl st in beg sc, turn.

Rnd 3: Ch 1, sc in each st and in each ch-1 sp around, join with sl st in beg sc, fasten off. ❖

TROPICAL COLORS PURSE CONTINUED FROM PAGE 11

around fpdc directly below, sc in next sc] across, turn.

Row 36: Ch 1, sc in each of next 21 sts, turn.

Rows 37 & 38: Rep rows 35 and 36.

Row 39: Rep row 35, fasten off.

2nd Top Shaping
Row 34 (WS): Sk next st, attach CC in next st, ch 1, sc in same st, sc in each of next 20 sts, turn. *(21 sc)*
Row 35 (RS): Rep row 35 of First Top Shaping.
Rows 36–39: Rep rows 36–39 of First Top Shaping.

Attaching Handles
With WS facing, fold First Top Shaping over bamboo handle to inside of Purse and sew across edge. Attach 2nd bamboo handle on 2nd Top Shaping in same manner.

Embellishment
With 1 strand of CC, make a ch approximately 60 inches long. Sew ch to center MC section of Purse making lps and waves on both sides. ❧

NEON STRIPES SCARF CONTINUED FROM PAGE 16

Row 6: Rep row 2.
Row 7: Rep row 3, change color to watermelon in last st, turn.
Row 8: Rep row 2.
Row 9: Rep row 3, change color to mango in last st, turn.
Row 10: Rep row 2.
Row 11: Rep row 3, change color to lemonade in last st, turn.
Row 12: Rep row 2.
Row 13: Rep row 3, change color to watermelon in last st, turn.
Row 14: Rep row 2.
Row 15: Ch 1, sc in each st across, fasten off.

Trim
Row 1: With RS facing, working in ends of rows, attach watermelon with sl st in end of first row, ch 1, sc evenly sp across, fasten off. *(21 sc)*
Rep row 1 of Trim on opposite end of Scarf.

Fringe
Work Fringe in each end of Scarf in row 1 of Trim. For each Fringe, cut 1 strand each watermelon, lemonade and mango, each 16 inches long. Holding 3 strands tog, fold in half, insert hook in sc st, draw strands through at fold to form a lp on hook, draw cut ends through lp on hook, pull gently to tighten. ❧

ILLUSION TOP CONTINUED FROM PAGE 17

Pattern Notes
Weave in loose ends as work progresses.
Join rounds with a slip stitch unless otherwise stated.

Special Stitches
Shell: 5 dc in indicated st.
Beginning shell (beg shell): Ch 3, 2 dc in same sc as beg ch-3.

Bodice
Rnd 1: With pink, ch 70 [75, 80], sl st to join in first ch to form a ring, ch 3 *(counts as first dc)*, dc in each of next 3 chs, 2 dc in next ch, [dc in each of next 4 chs, 2 dc in next ch] 13 [13, 14] times, dc in each of next 0 [5, 5] chs, join in 3rd ch of beg ch-3. *(84 [89, 95] dc)*
Rnd 2: Working in **front lp** *(see Stitch Guide)* of each st for this rnd only, dc around, inc 14 [14, 15] dc evenly sp around, join in 3rd ch of beg ch-3. *(98 [103, 110] dc)*
Rnd 3: Ch 3, dc in each dc around, join in 3rd ch of beg ch-3.
Rnds 4–7: Rep rnd 3.
Rnd 8: Ch 3, dc in each of next 13 [14, 15] dc, sk next 21 [22, 23] dc *(armhole)*, dc in each of next 28 [29, 21] dc, sk next 21 [22, 23] dc *(armhole)* dc in next 14 [15,

16] dc, join in 3rd ch of beg ch-3. *(56 [59, 64] dc)*

Rnds 9–16 [9–17, 9–18]: Rep rnd 3.

Rnd 17 [18, 19]: Ch 3, working in front lps only, dc in each st around, join in 3rd ch of beg ch-3, fasten off.

Rnd 18 [19, 20]: Attach 3 strands of variegated cotton in rem free lp of rnd 16 [17, 18], ch 1, sc in same st as beg ch-1, *sk next st, **shell** *(see Special Stitches)* in next st, sk next st**, sc in next st, rep from * around, ending last rep at **, join in beg sc, turn. *(14 [15, 16] shells)*

Rnd 19 [20, 21]: Work **beg shell** *(see Special Stitches)*, *sc in center dc of next shell**, shell in next sc, rep from * around, ending last rep at **, 2 dc in same sc as beg shell, join in 3rd ch of beg ch-3.

Rnd 20 [21, 22]: Ch 1, sc in same dc as joining, *shell in next sc**, sc in center dc of next shell, rep from * around, ending last rep at **, join in beg sc.

Note: *To lengthen coordinating tank top, continue to rep rnds 19 & 20 [20 & 21, 21 & 22] to desired length.*

Rnd 21 [22, 23]: Ch 1, sc in each st around, join in beg sc, fasten off.

Sleeve

Make 2.

Rnd 1: Working in sk sts of rnd 7, attach pink in underarm st and sl st first and last st tog, ch 3, dc in each of next 21 [22, 23] sts, join in 3rd ch of beg ch-3. *(22 [23, 24] dc)*

Rnd 2: Ch 1, sc in same st as beg ch-1, sc in each dc around, join in beg sc, fasten off.

Front Yoke

Row 1: Find beg ch-3 of rnd 1 of bodice, attach 3 strands of variegated cotton in rem free **back lp** *(see Stitch Guide)* of 30th [33rd, 35th] st, ch 1, sc in same st as beg ch-1, [sk next 2 sts, shell in next st, sk next 2 sts, sc in next st] 5 times, turn leaving rem sts unworked. *(5 shells; 6 sc)*

Row 2: Beg shell in first sc, [sc in center of next shell, shell in next sc] 4 times, sc in next shell, 3 dc in last shell, turn.

Row 3: Ch 1, sc in first dc, shell in next sc, sc in center of next shell, turn leaving rem sts unworked. *(7 sts)*

Row 4: Beg shell in first sc, sc in center of next shell, 3 dc in last sc, turn.

Row 5 (sizes 5 & 6 only): Rep row 3.

Row 6 (size 6 only): Rep row 4.

Row 7 (sizes 4 & 6 only): Sl st in each of next 3 sts, 3 dc in next sc, sc in last st, fasten off.

Row 7 (size 5 only): Beg shell in first sc, sc in center of next shell, sl st in last 3 sts, fasten off.

Row 8: Sk next 17 sts of row 2 of Front Yoke, attach 3 strands of variegated in next st, ch 1, sc in same st as beg ch-1, shell in next sc, sc in last st, turn. *(7 sts)*

Row 9: Rep row 4.

Row 10 (sizes 5 & 6 only): Rep row 3.

Row 11 (size 6 only): Rep row 4.

Row 12 (sizes 4 & 6 only): Ch 1, sc in first st, 3 dc in next sc, sl st in each of next 3 sts, fasten off.

Row 12 (size 5 only): Sl st in each of next 3 sts, sc in center of shell, 3 dc in last sc, fasten off.

Back Yoke

Row 1: Sk next 11 [13, 16] sts of rnd 1 of Bodice, attach 3 strands of variegated cotton in next st, ch 1, sc in same st as beg ch-1, [sk next 2 sts, shell in next st, sk next 2 sts, sc in next st] 5 times, turn. *(5 shells; 6 sc)*

Rows 2–12: Rep rows 2–12 of Front Yoke.

Assembly

Holding RS of shoulder straps tog, attach 3 strands of variegated cotton and working through both thicknesses, sl st in each st across, fasten off.

Neckline Trim

Rnd 1: Attach 3 strands of variegated cotton at shoulder seam, ch 1, sc evenly sp around neckline opening, join in beg sc, fasten off.

Arm Trim

Make 2.

Row 1 (RS): Attach 3 strands of variegated cotton in side edge of row 1 of Yoke, ch 1, sc evenly sp across ends of rows of arm edge. ❖

BUG RUG CONTINUED FROM PAGE 25

Rnd 8: Ch 3, dc in next st, [2 dc in next st, dc in each of next 2 sts] around, join in 3rd ch of beg ch-3. *(46 sts)*

Rnd 9: Ch 3, [2 dc in next st, dc in each of next 2 sts] 15 times, join in 3rd ch of beg ch-3. *(61 sts)* Stuff hat lightly with fiberfill and sew to head. Turn front brim up and tack in place. Center flower appliqué on brim and sew to hat. With needle and light blue ribbon outline Eyes and then fill with random seed sts until solid. With pink ribbon, embroider in same manner for cheeks. With hot pink ribbon, embroider Mouth in straight sts.

Antennae Circle
Make 14.

Rnd 1: With grass green, ch 3, sl st in first ch to form a ring, ch 1, 8 hdc in ring, join in top of first hdc, fasten off. *(8 sts)*

Stack 7 circles and sew tog through center of circles.

Antennae Topper
Make 2.

Rnds 1–3: Rep rnds 1–3 of Head with lime blue. *(18 sts)*

Rnds 4 & 5: Ch 1, hdc in each st around, join in top of first hdc.

Rnds 6 & 7: Ch 1, [hdc in next st, hdc dec in next 2 sts] around, join in first hdc. *(8 sts)*

Rnd 8: Ch 1, lightly stuff Antennae Topper and insert plastic squeaker, [hdc dec in next 2 sts] 4 times, join in top of first hdc, fasten off.

Sew an Antennae Topper to end of each Antennae Circle group. Sew antennas to each side of Head on Hat. Sew Legs evenly sp around outer edge of Body. ❧

EDWARD THE SWEATER BEAR CONTINUED FROM PAGE 27

At the end of Rnd 18, stuff Leg with fiberfill and continue stuffing as work progresses.

Rnd 19: [Sc in next st, sc dec in next 2 sts] around. *(14 sc)*

Rnd 20: [Sc dec in next 2 sts] around, sl st in next st, leaving a length of yarn, fasten off. *(7 sc)* Sew Leg to side of Body.

Ear
Make 2.

Rnd 1: Using sierra, ch 2, 6 sc in 2nd ch from hook. *(6 sc)*

Rnd 2: 2 sc in each st around. *(12 sc)*

Rnd 3: [Sc in next st, 2 sc in next st] around. *(18 sc)*

Rnd 4: [Sc in each of next 2 sts, 2 sc in next st] around. *(24 sc)*

Rnds 5 & 6: Sc in each st around. At the end of rnd 6, sl st in next st, leaving a length of yarn, fasten off. Flatten piece and sew to side of head near top.

Muzzle

Rnd 1: With sierra, ch 2, 6 sc in 2nd ch from hook. *(6 sc)*

Rnd 2: 2 sc in each st around.

Rnd 3: Sc in each st around.

Rnd 4: [Sc in next st, 2 sc in next st] around. *(18 sc)*

Rnd 5: Rep rnd 3.

Rnd 6: [Sc in each of next 2 sts, 2 sc in next st] around. *(24 sc)*

Rnd 7: Rep rnd 3, sl st in next st to join, leaving a length of yarn, fasten off.

Stuff lightly with fiberfill and sew Muzzle to Head centered below Eyes.

Finishing

With black yarn, embroider nose on Muzzle in satin st, embroider mouth directly below with straight st. ❧

L-EGANT
ACCENTS

Let your size L hook create some crochet magic with this fabulous collection of glamorous styles to dress up your wardrobe and home. A creative mix of fashion and ordinary yarns takes these projects from fun and fanciful to sumptuous and sensational!

MERMAID SHRUG

With its cool, airy design, this flirty and feminine ribbon-yarn shrug is the perfect warm weather cover-up for a pretty dress, tank top or camisole.

INTERMEDIATE

MEDIUM 4

Finished Sizes

Extra small/small [medium/large, X-large/2X-large]
Bust: 28 to 34 [36 to 44, 46 to 52] inches

Gauge

6 sc in front lps = 2 inches; 7 rows = 4 inches
Before measuring swatch, stretch firmly in both directions, then allow it to relax into shape naturally on a smooth surface.

Pattern Notes

Weave in loose ends as work progresses.
Join rounds with a slip stitch unless otherwise stated.
Shrug is crocheted in vertical rows as a flat piece.
All single crochet stitches are worked in front loops only unless otherwise specified.

Materials

- Red Heart Tiki medium (worsted) weight yarn (1¾ oz/157 yds/50g per skein): 3 [3, 4] skeins #3961 aruba
- Size L/11/8mm crochet hook or size needed to obtain gauge
- Tapestry needle
- Stitch markers

Shrug Body

Row 1: Ch 35 [35, 41] loosely, sc in **back bar** (see illustration) of 2nd ch from hook and in back bar of each ch across, place markers in first and last chs worked in, turn. (34 [34, 40] sc)

Back Bar of Ch

Rows 2–37 [2–40, 2–46]: Ch 1, sc in **front lp** (see Stitch Guide) of each st across, turn. At the end of last rep place markers in first and last sc of last row, do not fasten off.

First Sleeve

Rows 1–11 [1–13, 1–12]: Rep row 2.
Row 12 [14, 13]: Ch 1, sc in each of first 2 sts, **sc dec** (see Stitch Guide) in next 2 sts, sc in each st across, turn. (33 [33, 39] sc)
Rows 13–30 [15–32, 14–34]: Rep row 12 [14, 13]. (15 [15, 18] sts)
Fold piece in half lengthwise, loosely sl st ends of rows tog across to last markers placed, fasten off.

2nd Sleeve

Row 1: Working in opposite side of foundation ch of row 1, join with sl st in first marked ch, sc in each ch across to last marked ch, turn.

Rows 2–30 [2–32, 2–34]: Rep rows 2–30 [2–32, 2–34] of First Sleeve.

Fold piece in half lengthwise, loosely sl st ends of rows tog across to last markers placed, do not fasten off.

Body Trim

Rnd 1: Working in ends of rows across Body, ch 1, sc in end of each row around, join with sl st in beg sc, turn. Remove markers, leaving 1 to mark beg of rnd. *(74 [80, 92] sc)*

Rnd 2: Ch 1, sc in each of first 5 [6, 7] sts, sc dec in next 2 sts, *sc in each of next 5 [6, 7] sts, sc dec in next 2 sts, rep from * around, ending with sc in each of last 4 [0, 2] sts, join with sl st in beg sc, turn. *(64 [70, 82] sc)*

Note: *Work in continuous rnds, do not join or turn.*

Rnd 3: Sc in each of first 4 sts, sc dec in next 2 sts, *sc in each of next 2 [5, 4] sts, sc dec in next 2 sts, rep from * around, ending with sc in each of last 6 [1, 4] sts. *(50 [57, 69] sc)*

Rnd 4: Sc in each st around.

Rnd 5: Sc in first sc, ch 3, sk next 1 [2, 2] sc, [sc in next sc, ch 3, sk next 2 sc] around, sc in next st.

Rnd 6: [Ch 5, sk ch sp, sc in next st] around.

Rnd 7: [Ch 7, sk ch sp, sc in next st] around.

Rnd 8: [Ch 9, sk ch sp, sc in next st] around.

Rnd 9: [Ch 11, sk ch sp, sc in next st] around.

Rnd 10: [Ch 13, sk ch sp, sc in next st] around, fasten off.

Sleeve Cuff

Make 2.

Note: *Work in continuous rnds, do not join or turn.*

Rnd 1: Join with sc in Sleeve seam, [ch 5, sk next 2 sts, sc in next st] around to last 3 sts, ch 5, sk next 3 sts, sc in first sc, mark first st with st marker.

Rnd 2: [Ch 6, sk ch sp, sc in next st] around.

Rnd 3: [Ch 8, sk ch sp, sc in next st] around.

Rnd 4: [Ch 10, sk ch sp, sc in next st] around.

Rnd 5: [Ch 11, sk ch sp, sc in next st] around.

Rnd 6: [Ch 12, sk ch sp, sc in next st] around.

Rnd 7: [Ch 13, sk ch sp, sc in next st] around.

Rnd 8: [Ch 14, sk ch sp, sc in next st] around, fasten off. ❖

NIGHT & DAY JACKET

A subtle blend of black and white created with intermittent loops of color takes a classic look in a fanciful new direction in this cozy, ultra-chic jacket.

INTERMEDIATE

6
SUPER BULKY

4
MEDIUM

Finished Sizes

Small [medium, large, X-large, 2X-large]

Bust: 23–34 [36–38, 40–42, 44–46, 48–50] inches

Gauge

8 dc = 4 inches; 13 rows = 12 inches

Pattern Notes

Weave in loose ends as work progresses.

Join rounds with a slip stitch unless otherwise stated.

Special Stitches

Beginning double crochet decrease (beg dc dec):

Materials

- Patons Pooch super bulky (super chunky) weight yarn (2.4 oz/36 yds/70g per ball):
    13 [15, 17, 18, 20] balls #65046 lamb
- 4-ply medium (worsted) weight yarn:
    1 yd black
- Size L/11/8mm crochet hook or size needed to obtain gauge
- Tapestry needle
- Elan horn-shaped button #292368 by Gutermann: 3

Ch 2, dc in next st. On return row, work last st in last dc, do not work in beg ch-2.

Back

Row 1: With lamb, ch 38 [42, 48, 52, 56] dc in 4th ch from hook, dc in each rem ch across, turn. *(36 [40, 46, 50, 54] dc)*

Row 2: Ch 3 *(counts as first dc)*, dc in each st across, turn.

Row 3 [3, 3 & 4, 3 & 4, 3& 4]: Rep row 2.

Rows 4 & 5 [4 & 5, 5 & 6, 5 & 6, 5 & 6]: Beg dc dec *(see Special Stitch)*, dc in each st across to last 2 sts, **dc dec** *(see Stitch Guide)* in next 2 sts, turn. *(32 [36, 42, 46, 50] dc)*

Rows 6 & 7 [6 & 7, 7 & 8, 7 & 8, 7& 8]: Ch 3, dc in same st as beg ch-3, dc in each st across to last st, 2 dc in last st, turn. *(36 [40, 46, 50, 54] dc)*

Rows 8–14 [8–14, 9–16, 9–16, 9–16]: Rep row 2.

Shape Armholes

Row 15 [15, 17, 17, 17]: Sl st in first 4 [5, 6, 7, 8] sts, ch 3, dc in each st across to last 3 [4, 5, 6, 7] sts, leaving rem sts unworked, turn. *(30 [32, 36, 38, 40] dc)*

Row 16 [16, 18, 18, 18]: Beg dc dec, dc in each st across to last 2 dc, dc dec in next 2 sts, turn. *(28 [30, 34, 36, 38] dc)*

Rows 17–21 [17–21, 19–24, 19–24, 19–26]: Rep row 2.

First Shoulder Shaping
Row 22 [22, 25, 25, 27]: Ch 3, dc in next 7 [8, 10, 10, 11] sts dc dec in next 2 sts, fasten off. *(9 [10, 12, 12, 13] dc)*

2nd Shoulder Shaping
Row 22 [22, 25, 25, 27]: Sk next 8 [8, 8, 10, 10] sts for back neck, attach lamb in next st, beg dc dec, dc in each of next 8 [9, 11, 11, 12] sts, fasten off. *(9 [10, 12, 12, 13] dc)*

Left Front
Row 1: With lamb, ch 23 [25, 29, 31, 33] dc in 4th ch from hook, dc in each rem ch across, turn. *(21 [23, 27, 29, 31] dc)*

Row 2: Ch 3, dc in each st across, turn.

Row 3 [3, 3 & 4, 3 & 4, 3 & 4]: Rep row 2.

Row 4 (small & medium sizes only): Ch 2, dc in each st across to last 2 dc, dc dec in next 2 sts, turn. *(20 [22] dc)*

Row 5: Beg dc dec, dc in each rem st across, turn. *(19 [21] dc)*

Row 6: Ch 3, dc in each st across to last st, 2 dc in last st, turn. *(20 [22] dc)*

Row 7: Ch 3, dc in same st as beg ch-3, dc in each rem st across, turn. *(21 [23] dc)*

Row 5 (large, X-large and 2X-large sizes only): Beg dc dec, dc in each rem st across, turn. *([26, 28, 30] dc)*

Row 6: Ch 3, dc in each st across to last 2 sts, dc dec in next 2 sts, turn. *([25, 27, 29] dc)*

Row 7: Ch 3, dc in same st as beg ch-3, dc in each rem st across, turn. *([26, 28, 30] dc)*

Row 8: Ch 3, dc in each st across to last st, 2 dc in last st, turn. *([27, 29, 31] dc)*

Rows 8–14 [8–14, 9–16, 9–16, 9–16] (all sizes): Rep row 2. *(21 [23, 27, 29, 31] dc)*

CONTINUED ON PAGE 60

PLUSH PULLOVER

A lavish mix of several sumptuous bulky yarns creates the "plush" in this beautiful sweater stitched in the deep, soothing colors of a twilight sunset.

EASY

Finished Sizes

Small [medium, large, X-large)

Bust: 32–34 [36–38, 40–42, 44–46] inches

Finished Garment Measurements

Bust: 37½ [41, 44½, 48] inches

Length: 19½ [20, 20½, 20¾] inches

Sleeve: 15½ inches

Gauge

8 sts = 4 inches; 8 rows = 4 inches

Pattern Notes

Weave in loose ends as work progresses.

5
BULKY

6
SUPER BULKY

Materials

- Patons Be Mine bulky (chunky) weight yarn (1¾ oz/95 yds/50g per skein):
  4 [5, 6, 7] skeins #63320 lovely lilac (A)
- Patons Pooch super bulky (super chunky) weight yarn (2.4 oz/ 36 yds/70g per skein):
  6 [6, 7, 8] skeins #65310 purple sunset (B)
- Patons Divine bulky (chunky) weight yarn (3½/ 142 yds/100g per skein):
  2 [2, 2, 3] skeins #06144 divine blue (C)
- Size L/11/8mm crochet hook or size needed to obtain gauge
- Yarn needle

Join rounds with a slip stitch unless otherwise stated. Back and Front are worked vertically from side to side. Color sequence for pullover is 1 row A (1 row B, 1 row C, 2 rows A, 1 row C, 1 row B, 2 rows A) rep color sequence.

Back

Row 1 (RS): Beg at underarm with A, ch 26, sc in 2nd ch from hook, sc in each rem ch across, turn. *(25 sc)*

Rows 2–4 [2–4, 2–6, 2–8]: Working in color sequence, ch 1, sc in each st across, turn.

First Shoulder

Row 5 [5, 7, 9]: Ch 1, sc in each sc across, ch 17 [18, 19, 20], turn.

Row 6 [6, 8, 10]: With sl st on hook, insert hook in last ch just made, yo, complete as sc, sc in each of next 16 [17, 18, 19] chs, sc in each rem sc across, turn. *(42 [43, 44, 45] sc)*

Row 7 [7, 9, 11]: Ch 1, sc in each st across, turn.

Rows 8–14 [8–16, 10–18, 12–20]: Rep row 7 [7, 9, 11].

Back Neck

Row 15 [17, 19, 21]: Ch 1, sc in next 41 [42, 43, 44] sts, leaving last st unworked, turn.

Rows 16–30 [18–32, 20–34, 22–36]: Rep row 7 [7, 9, 11].

2nd Shoulder

Row 31 [33, 35, 37]: Ch 1, sc in each st across, ch 1, turn.

Row 32 [34, 36, 38]: With sl st on hook, insert hook in ch just made, yo, complete sc, sc in each rem st across, turn. *(42 [43, 44, 45] sts)*

Rows 33–40 [35–44, 37–46, 39–48]: Rep row 7 [7, 9, 11].

Underarm

Row 41 [45, 47, 49]: Ch 1, sc in first 25 sts, leaving rem sts unworked, turn. *(25 sc)*

Rows 42–44 [46–48, 48–52, 50–56]: Rep row 7 [7, 9, 11]. At the end of last rep, fasten off.

Front

Rows 1–14 [1–16, 1–18, 1–20]: Rep rows 1–14 [1–16, 1–28, 1–20] of Back.

Front Neck

Row 15 [17, 19, 21]: Ch 1, sc in each of next 34 [35, 36, 37] sts, leaving rem 8 sts unworked, turn.

Rows 16–30 [18–32, 20–34, 22–36]: Ch 1, sc in each st across, turn.

2nd Shoulder

Row 31 [33, 35, 37]: Ch 1, sc in each st across, ch 8, turn.

Row 32 [34, 36, 38]: With sl st on hook, insert hook in last ch just made, yo, complete as sc, sc in each of next 7 chs, sc in each rem st across, turn. *(42 [43, 44, 45] sts)*

Rows 33–44 [35–48, 37–52, 39–56]: Rep rows 33–44 [35–48, 37–52, 39–56] of Back.

Sleeve

Make 2.

Row 1: With A, ch 21 [23, 23, 25] sc in 2nd ch from

CONTINUED ON PAGE 61

PURPLE PASSION

Dance the night away in this glamorous top that shimmers in sparkling medium-weight yarn. Long post stitches add texture and interest to the design.

Finished Sizes

Small [medium, large, X-large]

Bust: 21–34 [36–38, 40–42, 44–46] inches

Finished Garment Measurements

Bust: 34¾ [39¼, 43¼, 47¾] inches

Gauge

[Sc, ch 1] 6 times = 3¾ inches

Pattern Notes

Weave in loose ends as work progresses.
Join rounds with a slip stitch unless otherwise stated.

Special Stitch

Shell: 5 dc in indicated st.

Materials

- Lion Brand Glitterspun medium (worsted) weight yarn (1¾ oz/115 yds/50g per ball):
    8 [9, 10, 11] balls #144 amethyst
- Size L/11/8mm crochet hook or size needed to obtain gauge
- Tapestry needle
- Large-eyed sewing needle
- 8mm purple faceted beads: 30 [36, 40, 46]

Body

Rnd 1: Starting at waist and working upward, ch 108 [124, 136, 152], join with sl st in first ch to form ring, ch 1, sc in first ch, ch 1, sk next ch, [sc in next ch, ch 1, sk next ch] around, join in beg sc, turn. *(54 [62, 68, 76] sc; 54 [62, 68, 76] ch-1 sps)*

Rnd 2: Ch 1, sc in first sc, ch 1, [sc in next sc, ch 1] around, join in beg sc, turn.

Rnds 3–20: Rep rnd 2.

Front

Row 1: Ch 1, sc in first sc, [ch 1, sc in next sc] 22 [25, 27, 30] times, turn. *(23 [26, 28, 31] sc; 22 [25, 27, 30] ch-1 sps)*

Rows 2–5: Ch 1, sc in first sc, [ch1, sc in next sc] across, turn.

Row 6: Sl st in next ch-1 sp, sl st in next sc, ch 1, sc in same sc as beg ch-1, [ch 1, sc in next sc] 20 [23, 25, 28] times, turn leaving rem sts unworked. *(21 [24, 26, 29] sc; 20, [23, 25, 28] ch-1 sps)*

Row 7: Sl st in next ch-1 sp, sl st in next sc, ch 1, sc in same sc as beg ch-1, [ch 1, sc in next sc] 18 [21, 23, 26] times, turn. *(19 [22, 24, 27] sc; 18 [21, 23, 26] ch-1 sps)*

Rows 8–18: Ch 1, sc in first sc, [ch 1, sc in next sc] across, turn.

First Shoulder

Row 1: Ch 1, sc in first sc, [ch 1, sc in next sc] 4 [5, 5, 5] times, turn. *(5 [6, 6, 6] sc; 4 [5, 5, 5] ch-1 sps)*

Rows 2–9: Ch 1, sc in first sc, [ch 1, sc in next sc] across, turn. At the end of row 9, fasten off.

2nd Shoulder

Row 1: Sk next 9 [10, 12, 15] sc and next 10 [11, 13, 16] ch-1 sps, join with sc in next sc, [ch 1, sc in next sc] 4 [5, 5, 5] times, turn.

Rows 2–9: Rep rows 2–9 of First Shoulder.

Back

Row 1: For first armhole, sk next 4 [5, 6, 7] sc and next 5 [6, 7, 8] ch-1 sps, join with sc in next sc, [ch 1, sc in next sc] 22 [25, 27, 30] times, turn leaving rem 4 [5, 6, 7] sc for 2nd armhole. *(23 [26, 28, 31] sc; 22 [25, 27, 30] ch-1 sps)*

Rows 2–7: Rep rows 2–7 of Front.

Rows 8–23: Ch 1, sc in first sc, [ch 1, sc in next sc] across, turn.

First Shoulder

Row 1: Ch 1, sc in first sc, [ch 1, sc in next sc] 4 [5, 5, 5] times, turn.

Row 2: Ch 1, sc in first sc, [ch 1, sc in next sc] across, leaving a length of yarn, fasten off.

2nd Shoulder

Row 1: Sk next 9 [10, 12, 15] sc and next 10 [11, 13, 16] ch-1 sps, join with sc in next sc, [ch 1, sc in next sc] 4 [5, 5, 5] times, turn.

Row 2: Ch 1, sc in first sc, [ch 1, sc in next sc] across, leaving a length of yarn, fasten off. Using tapestry needle, matching sts and sps of last row of Front and Back, whipstitch shoulders tog.

Skirting

Rnd 1 (small size only): Working in opposite side of foundation ch of rnd 1 of Body, join yarn with a sl st in any ch, ch 3 *(counts as first dc)*, sk next 2 chs, **shell** *(see Special Stitch)* in next ch, sk next 2 chs, [dc in next ch, sk next 2 chs, shell in next ch, sk next 2 chs] around, join in 3rd ch of beg ch-3. *(18 dc; 18 shells)*

Rnd 1 (medium and large sizes only): Working in opposite side of foundation ch of rnd 1 of Body, join yarn with sl st in any ch, ch 3 *(counts as first dc)*, sk next ch, **shell** *(see Special Stitch)* in next ch, sk next ch, [dc in next ch, sk next 2 chs, shell in next ch, sk next 2 chs] around, join in 3rd ch of beg ch-3. *([21, 23] dc; [21, 23] shells)*

Rnd 1 (X-large size only): Working in opposite side of foundation ch of rnd 1 of Body, join yarn with sl st in any ch, ch 3 *(counts as first dc)*, sk next ch, **shell** *(see Special Stitch)* in next ch, sk next ch, [dc in next ch, sk next 2 chs, shell in next ch, sk next 2 chs] around, join in 3rd ch of beg ch-3. *([26] dc; [26] shells)*

Rnd 2 (all sizes): Sl st to center dc of next shell, ch 3, 4 dc in same st, **fptr** *(see Stitch Guide)* around single dc between shells, [shell in center dc of next shell, fptr around next single dc between shells] around, join in 3rd ch of beg ch-3.

Rnds 3–9: Sl st to center dc of shell, ch 3, 4 dc in same st, fptr around next fptr, [shell in center dc of next shell, fptr around next fptr] around, join in 3rd ch of beg ch-3. At the end of rnd 9, fasten off.

Sleeve

Make 2.

Rnd 1: Attach yarn with sc in first sk st of armhole on rnd 20 of Body, [ch 1, sc in next sc] 3 [4, 5, 6] times, ch 1, working in row ends of Front and Back, [sc in next row, ch 1, sk next row] 26 times, join in beg sc, turn. *(30 [31, 32, 33] sc; 30 [31, 32, 33] ch-1 sps)*

Rnd 2: Ch 1, **sc dec** *(see Stitch Guide)* in next 2 sc, ch 1, [sc in next sc, ch 1] 22 [23, 24, 25] times, [sc dec in next 2 sc, ch 1] 3 times, join in beg sc, turn. *(26 [27, 28, 29] sc; 26 [27, 28, 29] ch-1 sps)*

Rnds 3–37: Ch 1, sc in first sc, ch 1, [sc in next sc, ch 1] around, join in beg sc.

Rnd 38 (small size only): Ch 1, sc in first sc, ch 1, sc in next sc, ch 1, [sc dec in next 2 sc, ch 1] around, join in beg sc. *(14 sc)*

Rnd 38 (medium size only): Ch 1, sc in first sc, ch 1, [sc dec in next 2 sc, ch 1] around, join in beg sc. *(14 sc)*

Rnd 38 (large size only): Ch 1, [sc dec in next 2 sc] around, join in beg sc. *(14 sc)*

Rnd 38 (X-large size only): Ch 1, sc in first sc, ch 1, [sc in next sc, ch 1] twice, [sc dec in next 2 sc, ch 1] around, join in beg sc. *(16 sc)*

Rnd 39: Ch 3, shell in next sc, [dc in next sc, shell in next sc] around, join in 3rd ch of beg ch-3. *(7 [7, 7, 8] dc; 7 [7, 7, 8] shells)*

Rnd 40: Sl st into center dc of next shell, ch 3, 4 dc in same st, fptr around next single dc between shells, [shell in center dc of next shell, fptr around next single dc between shells] around, join in 3rd ch of beg ch-3.

Rnds 41–47: Sl st into center dc of shell, ch 3, 4 dc in same st, fptr around fptr, [shell in center dc of next shell, fptr around next fptr] around, join in 3rd ch of beg ch-3. At the end of rnd 47, fasten off.

Collar

Rnd 1: Using sewing needle, string all beads onto yarn, with WS facing, attach with sc in first st on Back, [push up a bead, ch 1 over bead, sc in next sc] 8 [9, 11, 14] times, push up a bead, ch 1 over bead, working in rows ends of shoulder, sc in first row, [sk next row, push up a bead, ch 1 over bead, sc in next row] 5 times, push up a bead, ch 1 over bead, working in sts across front, sc in next sc, [push up a bead, ch 1 over bead, sc in next sc] 8 [9, 11, 14] times, working in row ends of 2nd shoulder, push up a bead, ch 1 over bead, sc in first row, [push up a bead, ch 1 over bead, sk next row, sc in next row] 5 times, push up a bead, ch 1 over bead, join in beg sc, fasten off. *(30 [36, 40, 46] sc)* ❖

PLUM PIZZAZZ SCARF & HAT

A blend of two luxurious medium-weight yarns gives a delicious texture and cloud-soft feel to this yummy hat and scarf worked in a quick, super-easy pattern.

EASY

4 MEDIUM

Finished Sizes

Scarf: 6 x 56 inches
Hat: Small to medium [large to X-large]

Materials

- Red Heart TLC Amore medium (worsted) weight yarn (6 oz/312 yds/170g per skein):
  1 skein #3908 raspberry
- Red Heart Symphony medium (worsted) weight yarn (3½ oz/310 yds/100g per skein):
  1 skein #4907 magenta
- Size L/11/8mm crochet hook or size needed to obtain gauge
- Yarn needle

Gauge

6 sts = 2 inches; 6 rows = 2 inches

Pattern Notes

Weave in loose ends as work progresses.
Join rounds with a slip stitch unless otherwise stated.

Scarf

Row 1: With 1 strand each raspberry and magenta,

CONTINUED ON PAGE 62

BEVERLY HILLS GLITZ

Plush yarns with a bit of sparkle give frou-frou style and glitzy glamour to these fun, fabulous scarves that will give you star appeal wherever you wear them!

GLAMOUR SCARF

EASY

BULKY

Finished Size
7 x 63 inches,
excluding Fringe

MEDIUM

Materials
- Moda Dea Prima bulky (chunky) weight yarn (1¾ oz/72 yds/50g per skein):
    3 skeins #3010 white (A)
- Moda Dea Frivolous medium (worsted) weight yarn (1¾ oz/ 83 yds/50g per skein):
    3 skeins #9976 tutti frutti (B)
- Size L/11/8mm crochet hook or size needed to obtain gauge
- Yarn needle

Gauge
8 sts = 4 inches; 8 rows = 4 inches

Pattern Note
Weave in loose ends as work progresses.

Scarf
Row 1: With A, ch 18, sc in 2nd ch from hook, sc in

each rem ch across, fasten off, turn. *(17 sc)*

Row 2: With B, ch 1, hdc in each sc across, fasten off, turn.

Row 3: With A, ch 1, sc in each hdc across, fasten off, turn.

Rows 4–119: Rep rows 2 and 3. At the end of row 119, fasten off.

Fringe

Fringe is worked in each of 17 sts on each end of scarf. Cut 34 lengths each of A and B, each 13 inches long. Holding 1 strand each A and B tog, fold strands in half, insert hook in st on end of scarf, draw strands through loop at fold to form a lp on hook, draw loose ends through st on hook, pull strands gently to secure. Trim ends as desired.

GLITZ SCARF

EASY

5 BULKY

4 MEDIUM

Finished Size

6 x 63 inches,
    excluding Fringe

Materials

- Moda Dea Prima bulky (chunky) weight yarn (1¾ oz/72 yds/50g per skein):
    3 skeins #3622 olive
- Moda Dea Frivolous medium (worsted) weight yarn (1¾ oz/83 yds/50g per skein):
    3 skeins #9973 nightlife
- Size L/11/8mm crochet hook or size needed to obtain gauge
- Yarn needle

Gauge

6 sts = 2½ inches; 6 rows = 2½ inches

Pattern Note

Weave in loose ends as work progresses.

Scarf

Row 1: Holding 1 strand each olive and nightlife tog, ch 14, sc in 2nd ch from hook, sc in each rem ch across, turn. *(13 sc)*

Row 2: Ch 1, sc in each of next 3 sts, [ch 1, sk next sc, sc in each of next 2 sc] 3 times, sc in last sc, turn. *(10 sc; 3 ch-1 sps)*

Row 3: Ch 1, sc in each of next 3 sc, [ch 1, sk next ch-1 sp, sc in each of next 2 sc] 3 times, sc in last sc, turn.

Row 4: Ch 1, sc in each of next 3 sc, [dc in next corresponding sc 3 rows below, drawing dc up level with working row, sc in each of next 2 sc] across, ending with sc in last sc, turn.

Row 5: Ch 1, sc in each of next 3 sc, [ch 1, sk next dc, sc in each of next 2 sc] 3 times, sc in last sc, turn.

Row 6: Rep row 3.

Rows 7–138: Rep rows 4–6. At the end of last rep, fasten off.

Fringe

Fringe is worked in each of 13 sts on each end of scarf. Cut 26 lengths of each of olive and nightlife, each 13 inches long. Holding 1 strand each olive and nightlife tog, fold strands in half, insert hook in st on end of scarf, draw strands through at fold to form a lp on hook, draw loose ends through st on hook, pull strands gently to secure. Trim ends as desired. ❖

CITY CHIC PURSE

A combination of feathery eyelash and self-striping wool-blend bulky yarns creates a bold fashion statement in this fun, colorful go-anywhere purse.

INTERMEDIATE

5 BULKY

Finished Size
11 x 11 inches, excluding
   Handles

Materials
- Reynolds Smile bulky (chunky) weight yarn (124 yds/100g per skein):
    1 skein #205 variegated brown, bright green and fuchsia
- Schachenmayr Brazilia bulky (chunky) weight eyelash yarn (1¾ oz/99 yds/50g per skein):
    1 skein #21 chartreuse
- Sizes E/43.5mm and L/11/8mm crochet hooks or size needed to obtain gauge
- Tapestry needle
- Sunbelt purse handles: 2 lime green (P35 series)
- Stitch marker
- Decorative brooch (optional)

Gauge
Size L hook and variegated: rnds 1 & 2 = 4 inches; 5 sts = 2 inches

Pattern Notes
Weave in loose ends as work progresses.
Join rounds with a slip stitch unless otherwise stated.

Purse
Rnd 1: With size L hook, leaving a slight length of variegated at beg, ch 5, sl st in first ch to form a ring, working over ring and rem beg length, ch 3 *(counts as first dc)*, 14 dc in ring, join in 3rd ch of beg ch-3. Pull rem beg length to close opening, secure end and weave into piece. *(15 dc)*

Rnd 2: Ch 3, dc in same st as beg ch-3, 2 dc in each dc around, join in 3rd ch of beg ch-3. *(30 dc)*

Rnd 3: Ch 3, dc in same st as beg ch-3, dc in next dc, [2 dc in next dc, dc in next dc] around, join in 3rd ch

CONTINUED ON PAGE 62

SCARLET FEATHERS PILLOW

Add a flirty, feminine touch to your boudoir with this sassy red pillow stitched in sinfully soft yarn and woven through with strips of feathery mohair yarn.

INTERMEDIATE

Finished Size

14 inches square

5 BULKY

2 FINE

Materials

- Plymouth Sinsation luxury chenille bulky (chunky) weight yarn (1¾ oz/38 yds/50g per ball):
    3 balls #3375 red (A)
- Katia Ingenua fine (sport) weight yarn (1¾ oz/153 yds/50g per ball):
    2 balls #04 red (B)
- Size L/11/8mm crochet hook or size needed to obtain gauge
- Tapestry needle
- Sewing needle
- Sewing machine (optional)
- Red sewing thread
- 14-inch pillow form
- 15 x 29 piece coordinating red fabric

Gauge

[4 dc, ch 2] 4 times = 3½ inches; 2 rows = 2 inches

CONTINUED ON PAGE 63

MIDNIGHT MAGIC THROW

Plush, super-bulky chenille yarn gives this sumptuous throw velvety softness, and single crochet stitches worked in the back loops provides rich texture.

BEGINNER

SUPER BULKY

Finished Size

50 x 60 inches

Materials

- Sirdar Wow! chenille super bulky (super chunky) weight yarn (3½ oz/63 yds/100g per skein):
  19 skeins #762 blue indigo
- Size L/11/8mm crochet hook or size needed to obtain gauge
- Tapestry needle

Gauge

5 sc = 3 inches

Pattern Notes

Weave in loose ends as work progresses.
Join rounds with a slip stitch unless otherwise stated.

Throw

Row 1: Ch 86, sc in 2nd ch from hook, sc in each rem ch across, turn. *(85 sc)*

Row 2: Ch 1, working in **back lps** *(see Stitch Guide)* only, sc in each st across, turn.

Rows 3–106: Rep row 2. At the end of row 106, do not fasten off.

Border

Rnd 1: Working down side edge of row, [ch 3, sk 1 row, sc in next row] across *(54 ch-3 lps)*, working across opposite side of foundation ch, [ch 3, sk next ch, sc in next ch] across *(44 ch-3 lps)*, working across side edge of rows, [ch 3, sk 1 row, sc in next row] across *(54 ch-3 lps)*, working across row 106, [ch 3, sk next sc, sc in next sc] across, ending with ch 1, hdc in beg sc to form last ch-3 lp *(44 ch-3 lps)*. *(196 ch-3 lps)*

Rnd 2: Ch 1, sc in same sp as beg ch-1, [ch 3, sc in next ch-3 sp] around, ending with ch 1, hdc in beg sc to form last ch-3 lp.

Rnd 3: Rep rnd 2, fasten off. ❖

GOSSAMER THROW

The name says it all in this luxurious, light-as-air throw stitched in a blend of soft plush and mohair-type yarns that make it perfect for cool summer nights.

INTERMEDIATE

MEDIUM 4

Finished Size
45 x 64 inches

Materials
- TLC Amore medium (worsted) weight yarn (6 oz/278 yds/170g per skein):
    3 skeins #3103 vanilla (A)
- Red Heart Symphony medium (worsted) weight yarn (3½ oz/ 310 yds/198g per skein):
    3 skeins #4907 magenta (B)
- Size L/11/8mm crochet hook or size needed to obtain gauge
- Yarn needle

Gauge
10 sts = 4 inches; 10 rows = 4 inches

Pattern Notes
Weave in loose ends as work progresses.
Throw is crocheted vertically.

Throw
Row 1: With A, ch 150, sc in 2nd ch from hook, sc in each rem ch across, turn. *(149 sc)*

Row 2: Ch 4 *(counts as first dc, ch 1)*, sk next st, dc in next st, [ch 1, sk next st, dc in next st] across, **change color** *(see Stitch Guide)* to B in last st, turn. *(75 dc; 74 ch-1 sps)*

Row 3: Ch 1, [sc in dc, working behind ch-1 sp, dc in sk st 2 rows below] across, ending with sc in 3rd ch of beg ch-4, turn. *(149 sts)*

Row 4: Ch 3 *(counts as first dc)*, [dc in next dc, ch 1, sk next sc] across, ending with dc in each of last 2 sts, change color to A, turn.

Row 5: Ch 1, sc in each of first 2 dc, [working behind ch-1 sp, dc in sk st 2 rows below, sc in next dc] across, ending with sc in last st, turn.

Rows 6–105: Rep rows 2–5.

At the end of row 105, change color to A.

Row 106: Ch 1, sc in each st across, fasten off.

Fringe
Work fringe in ends of rows. Cut 5 strands each 20 inches long for each fringe. Fold strands in half, with WS facing, insert hook into end of dc row of same color, draw strands through at fold to form a lp on hook, draw cut ends through lp on hook, pull gently to secure. Rep Fringe in each row matching row color. ❖

AZTEC DREAMS THROW

Rich desert colors reflect the beauty of the Southwest in this deliciously soft, luscious throw stitched in smooth, suede-like yarn in a pretty striped pattern.

INTERMEDIATE

5
BULKY

Finished Size
44 x 68 inches

Materials

- Lion Brand Lion Suede bulky (chunky) weight yarn (3 oz/122 yds/85g per skein):
    6 skeins #133 spice
    4 skeins #098 ecru
    3 skeins #178 teal
    2 skeins #126 coffee
- Size L/11/8mm crochet hook or size needed to obtain gauge
- Yarn needle

Gauge

10 sc = 4 inches; 10 rows = 4 inches

Pattern Note

Weave in loose ends as work progresses.

Throw

Rnd 1 (RS): With coffee, ch 96, sc in 2nd ch from hook, [ch 1, sk next ch, sc in next ch] across, turn. *(48 sc; 47 ch-1 sps)*

Row 2: Ch 1, sc in first sc, sc in next ch-1 sp, [ch 1, sk next sc, sc in next ch-1 sp] across, ending with sc in last sc, turn. *(49 sc; 46 ch-1 sps)*

Row 3: Ch 1, sc in first sc, [ch 1, sk next sc, sc in next ch-1 sp] across, ending with ch 1, sk next sc, sc in last sc, turn. *(48 sc; 47 ch-1 sps)*

Row 4: Rep row 2, fasten off, turn.

Row 5: With RS facing, attach ecru with sl st in first sc, ch 1, sc in same st, [ch 1, sk next sc, sc in next ch-1 sp] across, ending with ch 1, sk next sc, sc in last sc, turn.

Row 6: Ch 1, sc in first sc, sc in next ch-1 sp, [ch 1, sk next sc, sc in next ch-1 sp] across, sc in last sc, fasten off, turn.

Row 7: With teal, rep row 5.

Row 8: Ch 1, sc in first sc, sc in next ch-1 sp, [ch 1, sk next sc, sc in next ch-1 sp] across, ending with sc in last sc, turn.

Row 9: Ch 1, sc in first sc, [ch 1, sk next sc, sc in next ch-1 sp] across, ending with ch 1, sk next sc, sc in last sc, turn.

Row 10: Rep row 8, fasten off.

Rows 11 & 12: With ecru, rep rows 5 and 6.

Row 13: With spice, rep row 5.

Row 14: Rep row 8.

Row 15: Ch 1, working in **back lp** *(see Stitch Guide)* of each st, sc in each st across, turn. *(95 sc)*

Row 16: Ch 1, sc in each st across, turn.

Row 17: Ch 1, sc in each of next 3 sc, dc in free lp of

st 2 rows below next st, sk st behind dc, [sc in next 7 sc, dc in free lp of st 2 rows below next st, sk st behind dc] across, ending with sc in last 3 sc, turn. *(12 dc; 83 sc)*

Row 18: Ch 1, working in **front lp** *(see Stitch Guide)* of each st, sc in each st across, turn.

Row 19: Ch 1, sc in first 2 sc, 3 dc in free lp of dc 2 rows below, sk 3 sc behind 3-dc group, [sc in each of next 5 sc, 3 dc in free lp of dc 2 rows below, sk 3 sc behind 3-dc group] across to last 2 sts, sc in each of next 2 sc, turn. *(12 groups 3-dc; 59 sc)*

Row 20: Ch 1, sc in first 3 sts, dc in center sk sc 2 rows below, [sk sc behind dc just worked, sc in each of next 7 sts, dc in center sk sc 2 rows below] across to last 3 sts, sc in each of next 3 sts, turn.

Row 21: Ch 1, sc in first 4 sts, [dc in free lp of center dc of 3-dc group 2 rows below, sk next sc behind dc, sc in next 7 sts] across, ending with dc in free lp of center dc of 3-dc group 2 rows below, sk next sc behind dc, sc in last 2 sc, turn.

Row 22: Ch 1, working in front lp, sc in each st across, turn.

Row 23: Ch 1, sc in first sc, [ch 1, sk next sc, sc in next sc] across, turn.

Row 24: Ch 1, sc in first sc, sc in next ch-1 sp, [ch 1, sk next sc, sc in next ch-1 sp] across, ending with sc in last sc, fasten off, turn.

Rows 25 & 26: With ecru, rep rows 5 and 6.

Rows 27–30: With teal, rep rows 7–10. At the end of row 30, fasten off, turn.

Rows 31 & 32: With ecru, rep rows 5 and 6. At the end of row 32, fasten off, turn.

Row 33: With coffee, rep row 5.

Rows 34–36: Rep rows 2–4. At the end of row 36, fasten off, turn.

Rows 37–164: [Rep rows 5–36] 4 times. ✤

LUXURIOUS MOSAIC THROW

Creamy, wool-blend squares accented with a multitude of chic, colorful yarns make this a great project for using up all those leftover fashion-yarn scraps.

INTERMEDIATE

5 BULKY

Finished Sizes
Afghan: 53 x 63 inches
Motif: 4½ inches square

Gauge
Rows 1–7 of motif = 4 inches

Pattern Notes
Weave in loose ends as work progresses.
Join rounds with a slip stitch unless otherwise stated.
Two lighter weight yarns can be held together to approximate bulky weight yarn, as long as motifs are all the same size.

Motif
Make 128.
Row 1: With first scrap color, ch 2, 3 sc in 2nd ch from

Materials
• Lion Brand Wool-Ease Chunky bulky (chunky) weight wool-blend yarn (5 oz/153 yds/140g per skein):
    6 skeins #099 fisherman
• 40 oz assorted scrap bulky weight fashion yarns
• Size L/11/8mm crochet hook or size needed to obtain gauge
• Yarn needle

hook, turn. *(3 sc)*
Row 2: Ch 1, sc in first sc, 3 sc in next sc *(for corner)*, sc in next sc, turn. *(5 sc)*
Row 3: Ch 1, sc in each of next 2 sc, 3 sc in center corner sc, sc in each of next 2 sc, turn. *(7 sc)*
Row 4: Ch 1, sc in each of next 3 sc, 3 sc in center corner sc, sc in each of next 3 sc, **change color** *(see Stitch Guide)* to next scrap color, turn. *(9 sc)*
Row 5: Ch 1, sc in each of next 4 sc, 3 sc in center corner sc, sc in each of next 4 sc, turn. *(11 sc)*
Row 6: Ch 1, sc in each of next 5 sc, 3 sc in center corner sc, sc in each of next 5 sc, change color to next scrap color, turn. *(13 sc)*
Row 7: Ch 1, sc in each of next 6 sc, 3 sc in center corner sc, sc in each of next 6 sc, turn. *(15 sc)*
Row 8: Ch 1, sc in each of next 7 sc, 3 sc in center corner sc, sc in each of next 7 sc, fasten off. *(17 sc)*

Edging
Rnd 1 (RS): Attach fisherman in center corner sc of 3-sc group, ch 1, 3 sc in same st as beg ch-1, sc in each of next 7 sc, 3 sc in next sc, work 7 sc evenly sp down side edge of rows, 3 sc in opposite side of foundation ch, work 7 sc evenly sp up opposite side edge of rows with 3 sc in last row, sc in each of next 7 sc, join in beg sc, fasten off. *(40 sc)*

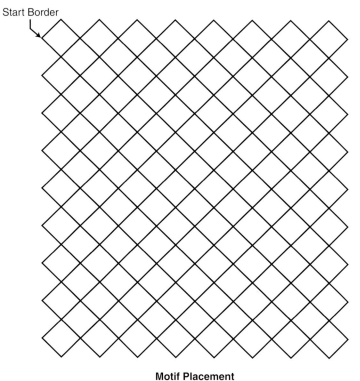

Motif Placement

Start Border

Assembly

With RS facing, working in **back lp** *(see Stitch Guide)* only of each st, whipstitch Motifs tog as indicated on motif placement chart.

Border

Rnd 1 (RS): Attach fisherman in center corner sc of 3-sc group as indicated on motif placement chart, ch 1, 3 sc in center corner sc to create and outside corner, *[sc in each of next 9 sc, **3-sc dec** *(see Stitch Guide)* in each of next 3 inside corners, sc in each of next 9 sc, 3 sc in next outside corner] 8 times, **sc in each of next 9 sc, 3 sc in corner**, rep between [ ] 7 times, rep between **, rep from * around, join in beg sc.

Rnd 2: Sl st in corner, ch 3 *(counts as first*

CONTINUED ON PAGE 63

NIGHT & DAY JACKET CONTINUED FROM PAGE 41

Shape Armhole

Row 15 [15, 17, 17, 17]: Sl st in first 4 [5, 6, 7, 8] sts, ch 3, dc in each rem dc across, turn. *(18 [19, 22, 23, 24] dc)*

Row 16 [16, 18, 18, 18]: Ch 3, dc in each st across to last 2 dc, dc dec in next 2 sts, turn. *(17 [18, 21, 22, 23] dc)*

Rows 17–19 [17–19, 19–21, 19–21, 19–23]: Rep row 2.

Neck Shaping

Row 20 [20, 22, 22, 24]: Sl st in first 7 [7, 8, 9, 9] sts, beg dc dec, dc in each rem st across, turn. *(10 [11, 13, 13, 14] sts)*

Row 21 [21, 23, 23, 25]: Ch 3, dc across to last 2 sts, dc dec in next 2 sts, turn. *(9 [10, 12, 12, 13] dc)*

Row 22 [22, 24 & 25, 24 & 25, 26 & 27]: Ch 3, dc in each st across, fasten off.

Right Front

Rows 1–3 (small & medium sizes only): Rep rows 1–3 of Left Front. *(21 [23] dc)*

Row 4: Beg dc dec, dc in each rem st across, turn. *(20 [22] dc)*

Row 5: ch 3, dc in next st, ch 1, sk next dc *(buttonhole)*, dc in each dc across to last 2 sts, dc dec in next 2 sts, turn *(19 [21] dc)*

Row 6: Ch 3, dc in same st as beg ch-3, dc in each dc across and dc in ch-1 sp, turn. *(20 [22] dc)*

Row 7: Ch 3, dc in each st across to last st, 2 dc in last st, turn. *(21 [23] dc)*

Rows 8–11: Rep row 2.

Row 12: Ch 3, dc in each st across to last 3 sts, ch 1, sk next dc *(buttonhole)*, dc in each of last 2 sts, turn.

Row 13: Ch 3, dc in next dc, dc in ch-1 sp, dc in each rem st across, turn.

Row 14: Rep row 2.

Shape Armhole

Row 15: Ch 3, dc across to last 3 [4] sts, leaving rem sts unworked, turn. *(18 [19] dc)*

Row 16: Beg dc dec, dc in each rem st across, turn. *(17 [18] dc)*

Rows 17 & 18: Rep row 2.

Row 19: Ch 3, dc in next dc, ch 1, sk next dc *(buttonhole)*, dc in each rem dc across, turn.

Neck Shaping

Row 20: Ch 3, dc in next 8 [9] sts, dc dec in next 2 sts, turn. *(10 [11] dc)*

Row 21: Beg dc dec, dc in each rem dc across, turn. *(9 [10] dc)*

Row 22: Ch 3, dc in each st across, fasten off.

Right Front

Rows 1–4 (large & X-large sizes only): Rep rows 1–4 of Left Front. *([27, 29] dc)*

Row 5: Ch 3, dc in each st across to last 2 sts, dc dec in next 2 sts, turn. *([26, 28] dc)*

Row 6: Beg dc dec, dc in each rem st across, turn. *([25, 27] dc)*

Row 7: Ch 3, dc in next st, ch 1, sk next dc *(buttonhole)*, dc in each rem st across to last st, 2 dc in last st, turn. *([26, 28] sts)*

Row 8: Ch 3, dc in same st as beg ch-3, dc in each rem st across, turn. *([27, 29] dc)*

Row 9: Ch 3, dc in each st across, turn.

Rows 10–13: Rep row 9.

Row 14: Ch 3, dc in each st across to last 3 sts, ch 1, sk next dc *(buttonhole)*, dc in each of next 2 sts, turn.

Rows 15 & 16: Rep row 9.

Shape Armhole

Row 17: Ch 3, dc in each st across to last [5, 6] sts, leaving rem sts unworked, turn. *([22, 23] dc)*

Row 18: Beg dc dec, dc in each rem st across, turn. *([21, 22] dc)*

Rows 19 & 20: Rep row 9.

Row 21: Ch 3, dc in next st, ch 1, sk next dc *(buttonhole)*, dc in each rem st across, turn.

Neck Shaping

Row 22: Ch 3, dc in each of next 11 sts, dc dec in next 2 sts, turn. *([13] sts)*

Row 23: Beg dc dec, dc in each rem st across, turn. *([12] sts)*

Rows 24 & 25: Rep row 9. At the end of row 25, fasten off.

Right Front

Rows 1–4 (2X-large size only): Rep rows 1–4 of Left Front. *([31 dc])*

Row 5: Ch 3, dc across to last 2 sts, dc dec in next 2 sts, turn. *([30] dc)*

Row 6: Beg dc dec, dc in each rem st across, turn. *([29] dc)*

Row 7: Ch 3, dc in each st across to last dc, 2 dc in last dc, turn. *([30] dc)*

Row 8: Ch 3, dc in same st as beg ch-3, dc across to last 3 sts, ch 1, sk next dc *(buttonhole)*, dc in last 2 dc, turn. *(31 sts)*

Row 9: Ch 3, dc in each st across, turn.

Rows 10–14: Rep row 9.

Row 15: Ch 3, dc in next st, ch 1, sk next dc *(buttonhole)*, dc in each rem dc across, turn.

Row 16: Rep row 9.

Shape Armhole

Row 17: Ch 3, dc in each st to last 7 sts, leaving rem sts unworked, turn. *([24] dc)*

Row 18: Beg dc dec, dc in each rem dc across, turn. *([23] dc)*

Rows 19–22: Rep row 9.

Row 23: Rep row 15.

Neck Shaping

Row 24: Ch 3, dc in each of next 12 sts, dc dec in next 2 sts, leaving rem sts unworked, turn. *([14] sts)*

Row 25: Beg dc dec, dc in each rem dc across, turn. *([13] dc)*

Rows 26 & 27: Rep row 9. At the end of Row 27, fasten off.

Sleeve

Make 2.

Row 1: With lamb, ch 37 [39, 43, 45, 51] dc in 4th ch from hook, dc in each rem ch across, turn. *(35 [37, 41, 43, 49] dc)*

Row 2: Ch 3, dc in each st across, turn.

Row 3: Beg dc dec, dc in each st across to last 2 sts, dc dec in next 2 sts, turn. *(33 [35, 39, 41, 47] dc)*

Rows 4–9 [4–9, 4–9, 4–9, 4–9]: Rep rows 2 and 3. *(27 [29, 33, 35, 39] sts)*

Rows 10–12 [10–12, 10–13, 10–13, 10–14]: Rep row 2.

Row 13 [13, 14, 14, 15]: Sl st in first 4 [5, 6, 7, 8] sts, ch 3, dc in each st across to last 3 [4, 5, 6, 7] sts, turn. *(21 [21, 23, 23, 25] sts)*

Row 14 [14, 15, 15, 16]: Beg dc dec, dc in each st across to last 2 sts, dc dec in next 2 sts, turn. *(19 [19, 21, 21, 23] sts)*

Rows 15 & 16 [15 & 16, 16 & 17, 16 & 17, 16–18]: Rep row 14 [14, 15, 15, 16]. *(15 [15, 17, 17, 15] sts)*

Row 17 [17, 18, 18, 19]: Beg dc dec, dc dec in next 2 sts, dc in each st across to last 4 sts, [dc dec in next 2 sts] twice, fasten off. *(11 [11, 13, 13, 11] sts)*

Finishing

Join shoulder seams, set in sleeves then join sleeve and side seams.

With black yarn, sew buttons opposite buttonholes.

Neck Edging

Attach lamb in st at top edge of Right Front neck edge, ch 1, sc evenly sp around neckline opening, ending with last sc in Left Front corner st, fasten off. ❧

PLUSH PULLOVER CONTINUED FROM PAGE 43

hook, sc in each rem ch across, turn. *(20 [22, 22, 24] sts)*

Rows 2–36: Work in color sequence, inc 1 st each end of row 8 [8, 4, 4] and every 4th row thereafter until there are 32 [34, 36, 38] sc. Work rem rows even in sc, ending with color A. At the end of last rep, fasten off.

Assembly

With yarn needle and A, sew shoulder seams, set in sleeves, sew side and sleeve seams.

Neck Edging

Rnd 1: Attach A with sc in right shoulder seam, ch 1, sc evenly sp around neckline edge, join in beg sc.

Rnds 2 & 3: Ch 1, sc in each sc around placing **sc dec** (see Stitch Guide) in 3 sc at each front corner, join in beg sc, fasten off.

Bottom Edging

Rnd 1: Attach A in side seam, ch 1, sc in each end of each row around bottom edge, join in beg sc.

Rnd 2: Ch 1, sc in each sc around, join in beg sc, fasten off. ❖

PLUM PIZZAZZ HAT & SCARF CONTINUED FROM PAGE 47

ch 170, sc in 2nd ch from hook, sc in each of next 8 chs, [ch 1, sk next ch, sc in next ch] 75 times, ch 1, sk next ch, sc in each of next 9 chs, turn. (169 sts)

Row 2: Ch 1, working in **back lps** (see Stitch Guide) of next 9 sts only, sc in each of next 9 sts, [ch 1, sk next ch-1 sp, sc in next sc] 75 times, working in back lps of next 9 sts only, sc in each of next 9 sts, turn.

Rows 3–19: Rep row 2. At the end of row 19, fasten off.

Hat

Row 1: With 1 strand each raspberry and magenta, ch 32, sc in 2nd ch from hook, sc in each of next 2 chs, [ch 1, sk 1 ch, sc in next ch] 11 times, [ch 1, sk 1 ch, sl st in next ch] 3 times, turn. (31 sts)

Row 2: Sl st in first sl st, [ch 1, sk next ch-1 sp, sl st in next sl st] twice, [ch 1, sk next ch-1 sp, sc in next sc]

11 times, ch 1, working in back lps only, sc in each of next 3 sts, turn.

Row 3: Ch 1, working in back lp of next 3 sts only, sc in each of next 3 sts, [ch 1, sk next ch-1 sp, sc in next sc] 11 times, [ch 1, sk next ch-1 sp, sl st in next sl st] 3 times, turn.

Rows 4–46 [4–48]: Rep rows 2 and 3, ending last rep with row 2.

Row 47 [49]: Holding opposite side of foundation ch together with last row and working through both thicknesses, ch 1, sc in each of first 3 sts, [ch 1, sk next ch-1 sp, sc in next st] 11 times, [ch 1, sl st in next st] 3 times, leaving a length of yarn, fasten off.

Weave rem length through sts across top edge of Hat, gently draw opening closed, knot to secure, weave length into side edge, fasten off. ❖

CITY CHIC PURSE CONTINUED FROM PAGE 50

of beg ch-3. (45 dc)

Rnd 4: Ch 3, dc in same st as beg ch-3, dc in each of next 2 dc, [2 dc in next dc, dc in each of next 2 dc] around, join in 3rd ch of beg ch-3. (60 dc)

Rnd 5: Ch 2 (counts as first hdc), working in **back lp** (see Stitch Guide) of each dc, hdc in each st around, join in 2nd ch of beg ch-2. (60 hdc)

Rnd 6: Ch 3, **fpdc** (see Stitch Guide) around next st, [**bpdc** (see Stitch Guide) around next st, fpdc around

next st] around, join in 3rd ch of beg ch-3.

Rnd 7: Ch 2, hdc in each st around, join in 2nd ch of beg ch-2.

Rnd 8: Ch 3, dc in each st around, join in 3rd ch of beg ch-3.

Rnds 9–11: Rep rnds 6–8.

Rnd 12: Rep rnd 6, fasten off.

Rnd 13: Attach 2 strands of bright green, ch 1, sc in each st around, join in beg sc, turn. (60 sc)

Rnd 14: Sc in each sc around, do not join, use st marker to mark rnds.

Rnds 15–18: Rep rnd 14.

Rnd 19: [With size E hook, draw yarn through opening at end of first handle, sc in next sc] 4 times, with size K hook, sc in each of next 10 sc, [with size E hook, draw yarn through opening at opposite end of first handle, sc in next sc] 4 times *(first handle completed)*, with size K hook, sc in each of next 12 sc, [with size E hook, draw yarn through opening at end of 2nd han-dle, sc in next sc] 4 times, with size K hook, sc in each of next 10 sc, [with size E hook, draw yarn through opening at opposite end of 2nd handle, sc in next sc] 4 times *(2nd handle completed)*, with size K hook, sc in each of next 12 sc, join in beg sc, fasten off.

Finishing

Attach decorative brooch between rnds 12 and 13 directly below handle. ❧

SCARLET FEATHERS PILLOW CONTINUED FROM PAGE 51

Pattern Note

Weave in loose ends as work progresses.

Pillow Cover

Fold matching red fabric in half, allowing ½-inch seam allowance, sew side seams. Insert pillow form, fold raw edges under and sew seam closed.

Pillow

Make 2.

Row 1: With A, ch 47, dc in 8th ch from hook, [ch 2, sk next 2 chs, dc in next ch] across, turn. *(15 dc; 14 ch-2 sps)*

Row 2: Ch 5 *(counts as first dc, ch 2)*, dc in next dc, [ch 2, sk next ch-2 sp, dc in next dc] across, turn.

Rows 3–14: Rep row 2.

Weave

Cut B into 280 pieces, each 30 inches in length: Divide into groups of 10 pieces per grid, weave over, under dc sts and through ch sps of grid, alternating the over and under bars, until all rows of grid are woven and leaving equal length on end of each weave. Turn 1 woven grid with end of weave at top and bottom and 2nd section with weave side to side. *Divide the 10 strands in half, insert 5 strands of 10-strand group of mohair under corresponding bar of opposite pillow piece, then holding all 10 strands tog, tie into a soft overhand knot. Rep from * on 3 sides of pillow, insert pillow form, then rep from * on rem side. ❧

LUXURIOUS MOSAIC THROW CONTINUED FROM PAGE 59

hdc, ch-1), ({hdc, ch 1} twice, hdc) in same st, *[ch 1, sk next sc, {hdc in next sc, ch 1, sk next sc} 4 times, yo, insert hook in next st, yo, draw lp through *(3 lps on hook)*, sk 3-sc dec, yo, insert hook in next st, yo, draw lp through *(5 lps on hook)*, yo, draw through all 5 lps on hook, ch 1, sk next sc, {hdc in next sc, ch 1, sk next sc} 4 times, (hdc, ch 1) 3 times, hdc in corner] 8 times, **ch 1, sk next sc, (hdc in next sc, ch 1, sk next sc) 5 times, ({hdc, ch 1} 3 times, hdc) in corner**, rep be-tween [ ] 7 times, rep from ** to **, rep from * ending with sl st in 2nd ch of beg ch-3.

Rnd 3: (Sl st, ch 3, sl st) in each of next 7 ch-1 sps, *[sl st in each of next 2 ch-1 sps, (sl st, ch 3, sl st) in each of next 11 ch-1 sps] 7 times, **sl st in each of next 2 ch-1 sps, (sl st, ch 3, sl st) in each of next 20 ch-2 sps**, rep between [ ] 6 times, rep bet **, rep from * around, join in beg sl st, fasten off. ❧

M-BELLISH THIS!

Embellishments in a variety of styles add decorative appeal to all types of fashions, accessories and home accents. From beads and tassels to shells and fringe, these fabulous finishing touches give winning style to the enticing projects included in this chapter.

SOMETHING TO TREASURE

A treasure in itself, this roomy tote is created in earth-tone neutrals and dressed up with pretty ribbon fringe. An abalone shell closure adds the beauty of the sea.

EASY

5 BULKY

Finished Size

11½ inches square, excluding
  Shoulder Strap and Fringe

Materials

- Lion Brand Homespun bulky (chunky) weight yarn (6 oz/185 yds/170g per skein):
    2 skeins #335 prairie
- Size M/13/9mm crochet hook or size needed to obtain gauge
- Tapestry needle
- Rayon seam binding:
  9 yds brick red
  6 yds each neutral green and spruce blue
- Rayon ribbon:
  2 yds each neutral green spruce blue and brick red
- Abalone shell with 2 holes

Gauge

5 sc = 2 inches; 6 rows = 2 inches

Pattern Notes

Weave in loose ends as work progresses.
Join rounds with a slip stitch unless otherwise stated.

Tote

Row 1: With prairie, ch 30, sc in 2nd ch from hook, sc in each rem ch across, turn. *(29 sc)*

Row 2: Ch 1, sc in each sc across, turn.

Rep row 2 until piece measures 23 inches from beg.

Row 3: Ch 1, sc in each of next 10 sc, ch 9, sk next 9 sc *(closure opening)*, sc in each of next 10 sc, turn.

Row 4: Ch 1, sc in each of next 10 sc, sc in each of next 9 chs, sc in each of next 10 sc, turn.

Rep row 2 until piece measures 6 inches from opening for closure piece.

CONTINUED ON PAGE 87

PRIMA DONNA NECKLACE

Bright beads and sassy tassels dress up your neck the way a scarf never could. This chic necklace will add pizzazz to any outfit from daytime casual to evening fun.

 EASY

 5 BULKY

Finished Size

54 inches, excluding 6–6½-inch Beaded Tassel on each end

Materials

- Moda Dea Prima bulky (chunky) weight yarn (1¾ oz/72 yds/50g per skein): 0.4 oz/ 19 yds/12g #3527 turquoise
- Moda Dea Bow Ties bulky (chunky) weight yarn (1¾ oz/64 yds/50g per skein): 0.4 oz/19 yds/12g #3741 calypso
- Size M/13/9mm crochet hook or size needed to obtain gauge

Gauge

4 chs = 2 inches

- Tapestry needle
- Bead needle
- Filament stringing beads
- Better Beads: BB8650-40 turquoise (600 count), BB8651-40 turquoise (100 count), BB8649-40 turquoise (100 count)
- Elite Better beads: BB10263-40 (8 count pack)
- Blue Moon Beads Art Glass: 2 glass pendant blue drop
- Bead Heaven: Light sapphire window & spacer beads Z13 (22 count window beads and 15g of matte spacers)

CONTINUED ON PAGE 87

FEATHER SOFT WRAP

Transform into a fashion maven when you wrap yourself in this majestic piece stitched in smooth and feathery yarns and accented with elegant beaded fringe.

INTERMEDIATE

4 MEDIUM

Finished Size

15 x 62 inches, excluding
Beaded Fringe

Materials

- Caron Simply Soft medium
  (worsted) weight yarn
  (6 oz/330 yds per skein):
    4 skeins #9738 violet
    7 balls #81305 parrot
- Sizes H/8/5mm and M/13/
  9mm crochet hooks or size
  needed to obtain gauge
- Tapestry needle
- Bead needle
- J & P Coats Dual Duty
  Plus purple extra strong
  sewing thread
- 5mm small oval purple
  glass beads: 200
- 5mm medium round
  purple glass beads: 200
- 10mm large oval purple
  glass beads: 100
- 4mm white pearls: 520

Gauge

Size M hook: 7 dc = 3 inches; 5 rows = 4 inches

Pattern Notes

Weave in loose ends as work progresses.
Work with 1 strand each violet and parrot held together throughout.

Wrap

Row 1 (WS): With size M hook and 1 strand each violet and parrot held tog, ch 34, dc in 4th ch from hook, dc in each rem ch across, turn. *(32 dc)*

Row 2: Ch 3 *(counts as first dc)*, dc in next dc, [**fpdc** *(see Stitch Guide)* around vertical post of next dc, dc in each of next 2 dc] across, turn.

Row 3: Ch 3, dc in next dc, [**bpdc** *(see Stitch Guide)* around vertical post of next post st, dc in each of next 2 dc] across, turn.

Row 4: Ch 3, dc in next dc, [fpdc around vertical post of next post st, dc in each of next 2 dc] across, turn. Rep rows 3 and 4 until Wrap measures 62 inches from beg or to desired length, fasten off.

Beaded Fringe

String beads on 1 strand purple sewing thread in the following sequence for each Beaded Fringe lp: *[4mm white pearl bead, 5mm oval purple bead] 5 times, [4mm white pearl bead, 5mm round purple bead]

CONTINUED ON PAGE 88

LACE SO SIMPLE

A whisper of crocheted lace around the shoulders gives the perfect touch of minimal coverage on soft spring or summer evenings.

INTERMEDIATE

MEDIUM

Finished Size

7½ x 54 inches, excluding crystals and fringe

Gauge

8 dc = 3 inches; 3 dc rows = 2 inches

Pattern Notes

Weave in loose ends as work progresses.
Lace is crocheted in a 27-stitch repeat; for additional length, chain number of stitches needed. Two additional teardrop crystals are needed for each additional repeat of length.

Materials

- Red Heart TLC Cotton medium (worsted) weight yarn (3½ oz/186 yds/100g per skein):
    1 skein #3001 white
- Size M/13/9mm crochet hook or size needed to obtain gauge
- Tapestry needle
- Sewing needle
- Sewing thread
- 9 teardrop crystals with lps for attaching

Special Stitch

Picot: Ch 4, sl st in first ch of ch-4.

Lace

Row 1: Ch 131, dc in 3rd ch from hook, dc in each rem ch across, turn. *(130 dc)*

Row 2: Ch 2 *(counts as first dc)*, dc in each of next 5 sts, *ch 7, sk next 6 sts, sc in each of next 3 sts, ch 7, sk next 6 sts**, dc in each of next 11 sts, rep from * across, ending last rep at **, dc in each of next 6 sts, leaving rem sts unworked, turn.

Row 3: Sl st into 4th st, ch 2, dc in each of next 2 dc, dc in each of next 3 chs, *ch 6, sk next 4 chs, sk next sc, sc in next sc, ch 6, sk next sc and next 4 chs, dc in each of next 3 chs, dc in each of next 3 dc**, ch 15, sk next 5 dc, dc in each of next 3 dc, dc in each of next 3 chs, rep from * across, ending last rep at **, turn.

Row 4: Sl st into 4th st, ch 2, dc in each of next 2 dc, dc in each of next 3 chs, *ch 3, sk next 3 chs, next sc and next 3 chs, dc in each of next 3 chs, dc in each of next 3 dc**, ch 7, sk next 3 dc and next 7 chs, (3 dc, ch 4, 3 dc) in 8th ch, ch 7, sk next 7 chs and next 3 dc, dc in each of next 3 dc, dc in each of next 3 chs, rep from * across, ending last rep at **, turn.

Row 5: Sl st into 4th st, ch 2, dc in each of next 2 dc, 3 dc in next ch-3 sp, dc in each of next 3 dc, *ch 7,

sk next 3 dc, sk next ch-7 sp, dc in each of next 3 dc, (3 dc, ch 3, 3 dc) in ch-4 sp, dc in each of next 3 dc, ch 7, sk next ch-7 sp, sk next 3 dc, dc in each of next 3 dc, 3 dc in ch-3 sp, dc in each of next 3 dc, rep from * across, turn.

Row 6: Sl st into 4th st, ch 2, dc in each of next 2 dc, *ch 7, sk next 3 dc, sk next 7 chs, dc in each of next 6 dc, (3 dc, ch 5, 3 dc) in ch-3 sp, dc in each of next 6 dc, ch 7, sk next ch-7 sp and next 3 dc, dc in next 3 dc, rep from * across, turn.

Row 7: Ch 1, sc in same st as beg ch-1, **picot** (see Special Stitch), *sc in each dc and each ch across to center of ch-5 sp, work picot**, sc in each dc and each ch to center dc of next 3-dc group, work picot, rep from * across, ending last rep at **, sc in each dc and each ch to last dc, work picot, sc in last dc, fasten off. (9 picots)

Finishing

With sewing needle and thread, sew a teardrop crystal to each picot.

For fringe, cut 2 lengths of white each 11 inches long and attach to bottom lp of teardrop crystal, rep attaching fringe to each crystal. ❖

TROPICAL STRIPES BOLERO

Brightly colored berry beads add a little extra pizzazz to this cheery jacket that adds a touch of the tropics to your wardrobe on even the gloomiest of days.

INTERMEDIATE

5 BULKY

Finished Sizes

Small [medium, large, X-large]

Bust: 32–34 [36–38, 40–42, 44–46] inches

Finished Garment Measurements

Bust: 31¾ [35¾, 40½, 44½] inches

Gauge

Rows 1–5 = 3 inches; 8 dclp sts = 3 inches

Materials

- Moda Dea Metro bulky (chunky) weight yarn (3½ oz/124 yds/100g per skein):
    3 [4, 4, 5] skeins #9512 ocean
- Caron Pizazz bulky (chunky) weight yarn (1¾ oz/28 yds per skein):
    9 [12, 14, 17] skeins #0001 birthday
- Turquoise crochet cotton size 10: 50 yds
- Size M/13/9mm double-ended crochet hook or size needed to obtain gauge
- Tapestry needle
- Sewing needle
- 15mm berry beads: 19 [21, 24, 27]

Pattern Notes

Weave in loose ends as work progresses.
Join rounds with a slip stitch unless otherwise stated.

Special Stitches

Double crochet loop (dclp): Yo, draw up a lp around next vertical (or horizontal) bar, yo, draw through 2 lps on hook.

Work loops off (work lps off): Yo, draw through first lp, [yo, draw through 2 lps on hook] across.

Back Panel

Row 1: With ocean, ch 31, [yo, draw up a lp in next ch, yo, draw through 2 lps on hook] across. (30 dclp)

Row 2: With birthday, **work lps off** (see Special Stitches) hook across.

Row 3: Ch 2, **dclp** (see Special Stitches) around each vertical bar across, turn.

Row 4: With ocean, work lps off hook.

Row 5: Ch 2, dclp around each horizontal bar across, turn.

Rows 6–25 [6–25, 6–29, 6–29]: Rep rows 2–5 consecutively.

Rows 26–28 [26–28, 30–32, 30–32]: Rep rows 2–4.

Row 29 [29, 33, 33]: Ch 2, hdc in next horizontal bar

CONTINUED ON PAGE 88

BLUE FLASH SHAWL

Dazzle your way through any room with all the glitter of a disco ball in this brilliant shawl created in sparkling metallic yarn. You'll be the star of the party!

EASY

5 BULKY

Finished Size

17½ x 70 inches, excluding Fringe

Materials

- Patons Glittallic bulky (chunky) weight yarn (1¾ oz/61 yds/50g per skein): 10 skeins #66128 blue flash
- Size M/13/9mm crochet hook or size needed to obtain gauge
- Tapestry needle

Gauge

Rows 1–5 = 4¾ inches; 11 dc = 4 inches

Pattern Notes

Weave in loose ends as work progresses.
Join rounds with a slip stitch unless otherwise stated.

CONTINUED ON PAGE 89

DESIGN BY TAMMY HILDEBRAND

VEGAS NECKLACE

Add some high-rolling fun to a casual-chic outfit with a kicky crocheted necklace that features decorative dice beads. It's sure to be a winning look!

EASY

Finished Size
25 inches long

Gauge
5 sc = 2 inches

4
MEDIUM

Materials
- Lion Brand Glitterspun medium (worsted) weight yarn (1¾ oz/115 yds/50g per skein):
  - 6 yds #153 onyx
- Size M/13/9mm crochet hook or size needed to obtain gauge
- Sewing needle
- 20 plastic dice shaped beads
- Purchased clasp & hook

Pattern Notes
Weave in loose ends as work progresses.

With sewing needle, alternating bead colors, string dice-shaped beads onto onyx yarn.

Necklace
Row 1: With onyx, ch 80, sc in 2nd ch from hook, sc in each rem ch across, turn. *(79 sc)*

Row 2: Ch 1, sc in each of next 15 sc, [(sc, ch 3, draw up a bead, ch 3, sc) in next sc, sc in next sc, (sc, ch 1, draw up a bead, ch 1, sc) in next sc, sc in next sc] 12 times, (sc, ch 3, draw up a bead, ch 3, sc) in next sc, sc in each of next 15 sc, fasten off.

Using sewing needle, sew clasp at beg of row 1. Sew hook to opposite end of row 1. ❖

CRAYON COLORS TOTE

As colorful as the box of 64, this cherry tote is large enough to hold a variety of goodies. Basic stitches make it easy and super bulky yarn makes it sturdy.

INTERMEDIATE

SUPER BULKY

Finished Size

11½ x 15 inches, excluding Strap

Gauge

4 sc sts = 2 inches; 4 sc rows = 2 inches

Materials

- Red Heart Grandé craft super bulky (super chunky) weight yarn (solids: 6 oz/149 yds/170g per skein; multis: 4½ oz/104 yds/127g per skein):
    - 2 skeins #2319 cherry
    - 1 skein #2937 wow
- Size M/13/9mm crochet hook or size needed to obtain gauge
- Yarn needle
- 1½-inch buttons: 1 each red, yellow and blue
- Stitch marker

Pattern Notes

Weave in loose ends as work progresses.

Do not join rounds unless otherwise stated. Use stitch marker to mark rounds.

Tote

Rnd 1 (RS): With cherry, ch 23, 3 hdc in 2nd ch from hook, hdc in each ch across to last ch, 3 hdc in last ch, working on opposite side of foundation ch, hdc in each ch across, do not join, mark rnds with st marker. *(46 hdc)*

Rnd 2: [2 hdc in each of next 3 hdc, hdc in each of next 20 hdc] twice. *(52 hdc)*

Rnd 3: [2 sc in each of next 6 hdc, sc in each of next 20 hdc] twice. *(64 sc)*

Rnd 4: Sc in each sc around.

Rnd 5: Hdc in each sc around.

Rnds 6–19: Hdc in each hdc around.

Rnd 20: Sc in each hdc around.

CONTINUED ON PAGE 90

FANCY FOOT WARMERS

Chase away even the most stubborn of chills with these chunky crocheted warmers that are more slippers than socks. Tassel accents add fringy fun.

INTERMEDIATE

5 BULKY

Finished Sizes

Ladies sizes: medium [large]

Materials
- Bulky (chunky) weight yarn (8 oz/325 yds per skein):
  - 2 skeins variegated red & purples
- Sizes G/6/4mm and M/13/9mm crochet hooks or size needed to obtain gauge
- Tapestry needle
- Stitch markers

Gauge
Size M hook: 4 sc rnds = 1½ inches; 3 sc = 1 inch

Pattern Notes
Weave in loose ends as work progresses.
Join rounds with a slip stitch unless otherwise stated.
Work with 2 strands held together throughout unless otherwise indicated.

Sock
Make 2.
Rnd 1 (RS): With size M hook, beg at top of sock, holding 2 strands of yarn tog, ch 24, sl st to join to form a

CONTINUED ON PAGE 90

FLIGHTS OF FANCY HAT & SCARF

Fly through your day with all the ease of a runway beauty when you top off your attire with this trendy set embellished with funky feathers!

EASY

MEDIUM

Finished Sizes

Scarf: 5½ x 51 inches,
    excluding Fringe

Hat: 9½ inches high x 20
    inches diameter

Materials

- 100 percent tweed wool medium (worsted) weight yarn:
    - 16 oz green tweed
    - 1 oz blue tweed
- Size M/13/9mm crochet hook or size needed to obtain gauge
- Tapestry needle
- Rayon seam binding: 3 yds forest green
- 4-inch peacock feathers: 3
- Craft glue

Gauge

5 dc = 2 inches; 4 dc rows = 3½ inches

Pattern Notes

Weave in loose ends as work progresses.
Join rounds with a slip stitch unless otherwise stated.

SCARF

Row 1: With green tweed, ch 17, dc in 4th ch from hook, dc in each rem ch across, turn. *(15 dc)*

Row 2: Ch 2 *(counts as first dc)*, dc in each st across,

change color *(see Stitch Guide)* to blue tweed, turn.

Row 3: Ch 2, dc in each dc across, change color to green tweed, turn.

Row 4: Rep row 2.

Row 5: Rep row 3.

Row 6: Ch 2, dc in each dc across, turn.

Rows 7–59: Rep row 6.

Row 60: Rep row 2.

Row 61: Rep row 3.

Row 62: Rep row 2.

Row 63: Rep row 3.

Rows 64 & 65: Rep row 6. At the end of row 65, fasten off.

Scarf Fringe

Working with green and blue tweed yarns and forest green seam binding, cut 8-inch lengths. Use 2 or 3 strands as desired, fold strands in half, insert hook into st of row 65 of Scarf, draw strands through at fold to form a lp on hook, draw cut ends through lp on hook, pull gently to secure. Work fringe in each st and in each st on opposite side of foundation ch of Scarf.

Neck Fringe

Mark off center 24 rows of Scarf, cut green and blue tweed yarns and forest green seam binding in 6-inch lengths. Using 2 strands as desired, fold strands in half, insert hook in end of row, draw strands through at fold to form a lp on hook, draw cut ends through lp on hook, pull gently to secure. Rep in each of rem 23 rows at neck edge.

HAT

Rnd 1: With green tweed, ch 5, sl st to join in first ch to form a ring, ch 2, 9 dc in ring, join in 2nd ch of beg ch-2, turn. *(10 dc)*

Rnd 2: Ch 2, dc in same st as beg ch-2, 2 dc in each rem dc around, join in 2nd ch of beg ch-2, turn. *(20 dc)*

Rnd 3: Ch 2, dc in same st as beg ch-2, 2 dc in each rem dc around, join in 2nd ch of beg ch-2. *(40 dc)*

Rnd 4: Ch 2, dc in each of next 2 dc, 2 dc in next dc, [dc in each of next 3 dc, 2 dc in next dc] around, join in 2nd ch of beg ch-2, turn. *(50 dc)*

Rnd 5: Ch 2, dc in each dc around, join in 2nd ch of beg ch-2, turn.

Rnds 6–11: Rep rnd 5. At the end of rnd 11, change color to blue tweed, turn.

Rnd 12: Rep rnd 5.

Rnd 13: Ch 1, sc in same dc, sk next 3 dc, [5 dc in next dc, sk next 2 dc, sc in next dc, sk next 2 dc] 7 times, 5 dc in next dc, sk rem 3 dc, join in beg sc, change color to green tweed, turn. *(40 dc; 8 sc)*

Rnd 14: Ch 1, sc in same sc as beg ch-1, sc in each st around, join in beg sc, fasten off. *(48 sc)*

Tassel

Cut several 14-inch lengths of each blue and green tweed yarns and forest green seam binding. Tie a length of yarn around the center of the bundle of strands, tie to center top of Hat. Glue each feather randomly to a strand of yarn. ❧

DESIGN BY CHRISTINE GRAZIOSO MOODY

SHADES OF THE SOUTHWEST

The spirit of the Southwest shines in this soft and cozy afghan created in bold rustic shades. Wooden beads add a traditional authentic touch.

INTERMEDIATE

BULKY

Finished Size

42 x 56 inches

Materials

- Lion Brand Homespun bulky (chunky) weight yarn (6 oz/185 yds/170g per skein):

  3 skeins #309 deco *(A)*

  1 skein #318 sierra *(B)*

  2 skeins #320 regency *(C)*
- Size M/13/9mm Tunisian crochet hook or size needed to obtain gauge
- Sizes G/6/4mm M/13/ 9mm crochet hooks or size needed to obtain gauge
- Yarn needle
- 100 count Mainstay Wood Pony beads #29004-02 (3 shades of beads): 3 packages

Gauge

4 rows tss = 2 inches; 4 dc of border = 2 inches

Pattern Notes

Weave in loose ends as work progresses.

Join rounds with a slip stitch unless otherwise stated. Row 1 of each panel is right side bottom edge.

Special Stitches

Tunisian simple stitch (tss): Insert hook under vertical thread, yo, draw up a lp.

Return: Yo, draw through first lp on hook, [yo, draw through 2 lps on hook] across until 1 lp remains on hook.

Afghan Panel

Make 4.

Row 1 (RS): With size M Tunisian hook and color A, ch 14, insert hook in 2nd ch from hook, yo, draw up a lp, [insert hook in next ch, yo, draw up a lp] across *(13 lps on hook)*, yo, draw through first lp on hook, [yo, draw through 2 lps on hook] across until 1 lp remains on hook.

Row 2: Tss *(see Special Stitches)* in each st across, **return** *(see Special Stitches)*.

Rows 3–87: Using graph as a guide, **change color** *(see Stitch Guide)* as indicated by graph, work tss across each row and return. At the end of row 87, do not fasten off.

CONTINUED ON PAGE 91

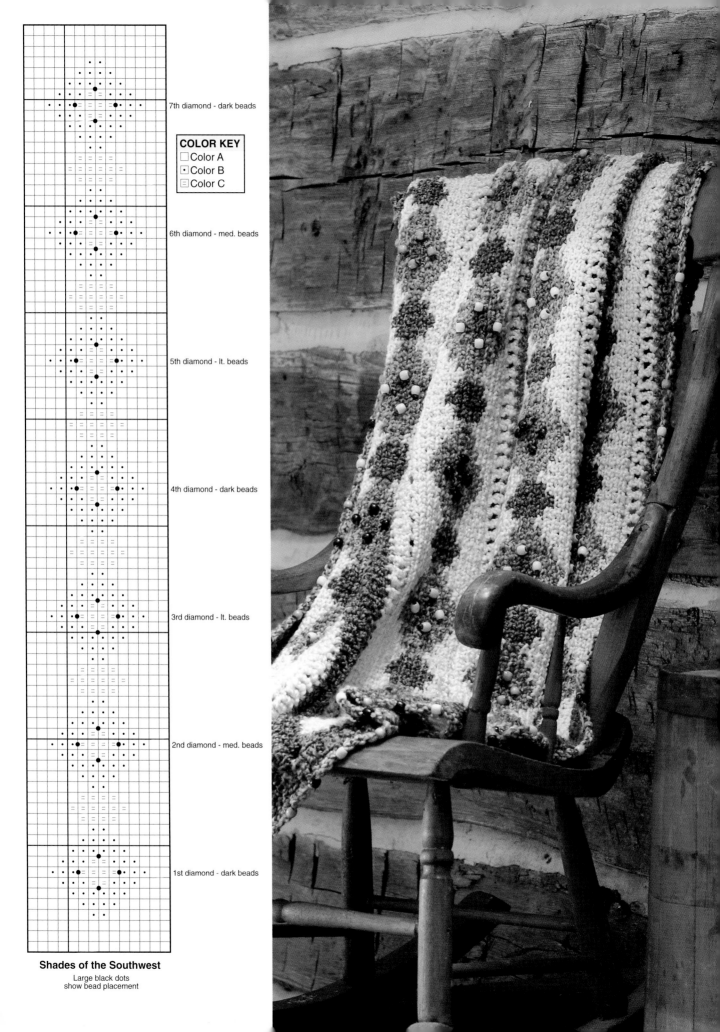

7th diamond - dark beads

COLOR KEY
☐ Color A
⊡ Color B
⊟ Color C

6th diamond - med. beads

5th diamond - lt. beads

4th diamond - dark beads

3rd diamond - lt. beads

2nd diamond - med. beads

1st diamond - dark beads

Shades of the Southwest
Large black dots
show bead placement

MIDNIGHT JEWELS AFGHAN

Rich and classic like your favorite heirloom necklace, this afghan features brilliant jewel tones and is accented with decorative, eye-catching fringe.

INTERMEDIATE

4 MEDIUM

Finished Size

45 x 68 inches, excluding Fringe

Gauge

2 rows = 2½ inches

Pattern Notes

Weave in loose ends as work progresses.
Work with 2 strands of yarn held together throughout.

Afghan

Row 1 (RS): With 2 strands of black held tog, ch 127,

Materials

- Red Heart Classic medium (worsted) weight yarn (solids: 3½ oz/190 yds/99g per skein; multicolors: 3 oz/167 yds/85g per skein):
    7 skeins #12 black
    3 skeins #959 gemstone
- Size M/13/9mm crochet hook or size needed to obtain gauge
- Yarn needle
- 7-inch square of cardboard

dc in 4th ch from hook, dc in each rem ch across, turn. *(125 dc)*

Row 2: Ch 3 *(counts as first dc)*, working in **back lp** *(see Stitch Guide)* for this row only, dc in each st across, turn.

Row 3: Ch 3, dc in each dc across, turn.

Rows 4 & 5: Rep rows 2 and 3.

Row 6: Rep row 2.

Topstitching

Row 1 (RS): Working with 2 strands of gemstone held tog, and leaving a 7-inch tail to be worked into fringe, attach gemstone with a sl st in **front lp** *(see Stitch Guide)* of 3rd dc of row 3, ch 1, sc in same sp as beg ch-1, *ch 5, sk next 5 dc of row 1, sc in front lp of next dc of row 1, ch 5, sk next 5 dc of row 3, sc in front lp of next dc of row 3, rep from * across, leaving a 7 inch tail, fasten off.

Row 2 (RS): Working with 2 strands of gemstone held tog, and leaving a 7-inch tail to be worked into fringe, attach gemstone with a sl st in same sp as first sc of previous row, *ch 5, sk next 5 dc of row 5, sc in front lp of next dc, ch 5, sc in same sp as next sc of previous row, rep from * across, leaving a 7-inch length, fasten off.

Finishing

*Beg with row 3 of Afghan, [rep rows 3 and 2] 3 times. Then rep rows 1 and 2 of Topstitching on the 6 rows of Afghan, rep from * 4 times (6 Afghan sections with Topstitching completed).

Fringe

Make 12.

Wrap gemstone around 7-inch cardboard 12 times, cut bottom edge of wrap, with strands folded in half, lp around gemstone sc at end of Topstitching, forming a lp on hook, draw cut ends and rem beg strands from Topstitching through lp on hook, pull gently to secure. Trim ends even. ❖

TRIPLE PLAY

Lounge around in style with this rich trio of luxurious throw pillows stitched in striking black and rose bouclé yarn.

INTERMEDIATE

5 BULKY

Finished Sizes

Square Diagonal Pillow:
15 x 15 inches, excluding Tassels

Rectangular Pillow: 14 x 18 inches, excluding Tassels

Bolster Pillow: 16 x 17½ inches, excluding Tassels

Materials

- Bernat Soft Bouclé bulky (chunky) weight yarn (5 oz/255 yds/140g per skein):
    4 skeins #06756 black
- Patons Divine bulky (chunky) weight yarn (3½ oz/142 yds/100g per skein):
    4 skeins #06430 richest rose
- Size M/13/9mm Tunisian crochet hook or size needed to obtain gauge
- Size L/11/8mm crochet hook or size needed to obtain gauge
- Large-eyed tapestry needle
- 14-inch square pillow form
- 12 x 16-inch rectangular pillow form
- 5 x 14-inch bolster pillow form
- 5½ x 8-inch piece cardboard

Gauge

Size M hook: 12 sts = 4 inches

Pattern Notes

Weave in loose ends as work progresses.
Join rounds with a slip stitch unless otherwise stated.
When working loops off hook, drop yarn to wrong side of work and work off next stitch with new color.

Special Stitches

Tunisian simple stitch (tss): Insert hook under vertical thread, yo, draw up a lp.

Return: Yo, draw through first lp on hook, [yo, draw through 2 lps on hook] across until 1 lp remains on hook.

Tassel

Make 10.

Wrap black yarn around 5½-inch width of cardboard 40 times. Tie a strand of black around all the threads at the top of the Tassel. Cut through all strands on the bottom of the Tassel. Wrap a strand of richest rose around Tassel several times about an inch down from top of Tassel, knot ends, tucking ends into the wrap. Use the long tails from the top of the Tassel to attach to Pillow as indicated.

SQUARE DIAGONAL PILLOW

Pillow
Make 2.
Row 1: With size M hook and black, ch 45, insert hook in 2nd ch from hook, yo, draw up a lp, [insert hook in next ch, yo, draw up a lp] across retaining all lps on hook, do not turn, **return** (see Special Stitches).
Row 2: First rem lp from previous row counts as first st of row, **change color** (see Stitch Guide) according to graph, work **tss** (see Special Stitches) across row, return.
Rows 3–34: Rep row 2.
Row 35: With black only, sk first vertical bar, [insert hook under next vertical bar, yo, draw through 2 lps on hook] across, fasten off.

Border
Rnd 1: With size L hook, attach black on first Pillow piece, ch 1, sc in each st around, join in beg sc, fasten off.
Rnd 2: Rep rnd 1 on 2nd Pillow piece.
Rnd 3: With size L hook, holding Pillow pieces WS tog

and working through both thicknesses, attach black, ch 1, sc across 3 sides of Pillow, draw up a lp, remove hook, insert square pillow form, pick up dropped lp and sc evenly sp across rem 4th edge, join in beg sc, fasten off. Attach a Tassel to each corner of pillow.

Square Diagonal Pillow

BOLSTER PILLOW

Row 1: With size M hook and black, ch 45, insert hook in 2nd ch from hook, yo, draw up a lp, [insert hook in next ch, yo, draw up a lp] across retaining all lps on hook, do not turn, return.
Rows 2–52: First rem lp from previous row counts as

first st of row, change color according to graph, work tss across row, return.

Row 53: With black only, sk first vertical bar, [insert hook under next vertical bar, yo, draw through 2 lps on hook] across, fasten off.

End Cap
Make 2.
Row 1: With size M hook and black, ch 10, draw up 1 lp *(2 lps on hook)*, to complete row, yo, draw through 1 lp, yo, draw through 2 lps.

Row 2: Draw up a lp in st just made, draw up lp in next ch *(3 lps on hook)*, to complete row, yo, draw through 1 lp on hook, [yo, draw through 2 lps on hook] across until 1 lp rem on hook.

Row 3: Draw up a lp in each of next 2 sts just made, draw up lp in next ch *(4 lps on hook)*, to complete row, yo, draw through 1 lp on hook, [yo, draw through 2 lps on hook] across until 1 lp rem on hook.

Row 4: Draw up a lp in each of next 3 sts just made, draw up a lp in next ch *(5 lps on hook)*, to complete row, yo, draw through 1 lp on hook, [yo, draw through 2 lps on hook] across until 1 lp rem on hook.

Row 5: Draw up a lp in each of next 4 sts just made, draw up a lp in next ch *(6 lps on hook)*, to complete row, yo, draw through 1 lp on hook, [yo draw through 2 lps on hook] across until 1 lp rem on hook.

Row 6: Draw up a lp in each of next 5 sts just made, draw up a lp in next ch *(7 lps on hook)*, to complete row, yo, draw through 1 lp on hook, [yo, draw through 2 lps on hook] across until 1 lp rem on hook.

Row 7: Draw up a lp in each of next 6 sts just made, draw up a lp in next ch *(8 lps on hook)*, to complete row, yo, draw through 1 lp on hook, [yo, draw through 2 lps on hook] across until 1 lp rem on hook.

Row 8: Draw up a lp in each of next 7 sts just made, draw up a lp in next ch *(9 lps on hook)*, to complete row, yo, draw through 1 lp on hook, [yo, draw through 2 lps on hook] across until 1 lp rem on hook.

Row 9: Draw up a lp in each of next 8 sts just made, draw up a lp in next ch *(10 lps on hook)*, to complete row, yo, draw through 1 lp on hook, [yo, draw through 2 lps on hook] across until 1 lp rem on hook, fasten off.

Note: *Rows 1–9 create a wedge.*
[Rep rows 1–9] 5 times *(total of 6 wedges for each End Cap)*, sew open edge and middle tog forming a circle.

Finishing
With size L hook and black, sc around each edge of the rectangle, then with WS tog and working through both thicknesses, sc the long edge tog. Fitting the End Cap to end with WS tog, sew or sc the End Cap into the opening. Insert bolster pillow form and sc or sew rem End Cap to opposite end of Bolster Pillow. Attach a Tassel to center of each End Cap.

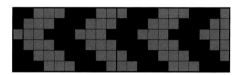
Bolster Pillow

RECTANGULAR PILLOW

Row 1: With size M hook and black, ch 50, insert hook in 2nd ch from hook, yo, draw up a lp, [insert hook in next ch, yo, draw up a lp] across retaining all lps on hook, do not turn, return.

Rows 2–73: First rem lp from previous row counts as first st of row, change color according to graph, work tss across row, return.

Row 74: With black only, sk first vertical bar, [insert hook under next vertical bar, yo, draw through 2 lps on hook] across, fasten off.

Finishing
With size L hook and black, sc around each edge of rectangle. With black and WS tog, matching stripes and working through both thicknesses, crochet both short edges tog, insert rectangular pillow form, sew or sc rem edge closed, fasten off. Attach a Tassel to each corner of Pillow. ❖

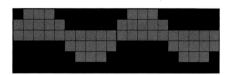
Rectangular Pillow

SOMETHING TO TREASURE CONTINUED FROM PAGE 66

Closure Flap

Row 1: Working on opposite side of foundation ch of row 1, sk next 11 chs, attach prairie in next ch, ch 1, sc in same ch, sc in each of next 7 chs, turn. *(8 sc)*
Row 2: Ch 1, sc in each of next 8 sc, turn.
Rep row 2 until Closure Flap measures 6 inches, fasten off.

Shoulder Strap

Row 1: With prairie, leaving a 9-inch length at beg, ch 80, sc in 2nd ch from hook, sc in each rem ch across, leaving a 9-inch length, fasten off, turn.
Row 2: Leaving a 9-inch length at beg, attach spruce blue seam binding, ch 1, sc in each sc across, leaving a 9-inch length, fasten off, turn.
Row 3: Leaving a 9-inch length at beg, attach prairie, ch 1, sc in each sc across, leaving a 9-inch length, fasten off, turn.
Row 4: With neutral green seam binding, rep row 2.
Row 5: Rep row 3.

Finishing

Place Tote on a flat surface with closure opening at the top, fold row 1 of Tote up to base of row 3 of closure opening.

Working through both thicknesses with neutral green, starting at row 1, sl st down side edge of Tote, leaving a 9-inch length for fringe, fasten off; rep sl st on opposite edge of Tote.

With brick red, leaving a 9-inch length at beg, sl st around flap of Tote and closure opening, leaving a 9-inch length, fasten off. With brick red, sl st across row 1 of Tote and around Closure Flap.

Attach abalone shell to Closure Flap with rayon ribbons. Attach as desired several strands of seam binding and rayon ribbons to shell closure. Attach Shoulder strap to each side of Tote.

Fringe

For fringe on bottom of Tote, including prairie and rem seam bindings and rayon ribbons, cut into 20-inch lengths and attach to bottom of Tote as desired. Fold a length in half, insert hook in bottom of Tote, draw strand through to form a lp on hook, draw cut ends through lp on hook, gently pull ends to secure.

PRIMA DONNA NECKLACE CONTINUED FROM PAGE 67

Pattern Note

Weave in loose ends as work progresses.

Necklace

Row 1: Holding 1 strand each turquoise and calypso tog, ch 50, fasten off.

Beaded Tassel

Make 2.

Make 3 strands of assorted beaded patterns, each approximately 12 inches long *(vary lengths for more visual impact)*.

Lay out 3 strands tog on a flat surface and using a 10-inch length of transite, tie strands tog in the middle of the lengths. Attach 1 of the fancier Elite Better Beads to each strand, adjusting the length to hang down inside the tassel.

Using another 10-inch length of transite, tie around the middle of tassel in the same place; attach 1 Blue Heaven Glass drops, adjusting the length to be the center piece of the tassel hanging down.

Use the opposite end of the transite to attach to end of Necklace. ❧

FEATHER SOFT WRAP CONTINUED FROM PAGE 68

5 times, [4mm white pearl bead, 10mm oval purple bead] 5 times, [4mm white pearl bead, 5mm round purple bead] 5 times, [4mm white pearl bead, 5mm oval purple bead] 5 times and 1 white pearl bead, rep from * 9 times to prepare beads for first end of Wrap. Each beaded Fringe lp will have 51 beads.

To join beads to lower edge of Wrap, with size H hook and RS of Wrap facing, join working strand of sewing thread with a sl st in first ch of Wrap, ch 1, 2 sc in same ch, 2 sc in next ch, *sc in next st in line with post st, push up 51 bead group, sc in same st as last sc, 2 sc in each of next 2 sts, rep from * across, fasten off. *(10 beaded fringe lps)*

Rep Beaded Fringe on opposite end of Wrap. ❖

TROPICAL STRIPES BOLERO CONTINUED FROM PAGE 72

and each horizontal bar to end, fasten off sizes small and large only.

Row [30, 34] (sizes medium & X-large only): Ch 2, hdc in each st across, fasten off.

Row [31, 35]: Working in bottom lps of row 1, attach ocean with sl st, ch 2, hdc in each lp across, fasten off.

Edging

Working in row ends of each odd numbered row and each hdc row, attach ocean with sc in first row, sc in same row, work 2 sc into each odd numbered row and hdc row to end, fasten off. Rep for 2nd side. *(30 [34, 34, 38] sc)*

Front Panel
Make 2.

Rows 1–5: Rep rows 1–5 of Back Panel.

Rows 6–9 [6–9, 6–13, 6–13]: Rep rows 2–5 of Back Panel.

Rows 10–12 [10–12, 14–16, 14–16]: Rep rows 2–4 of Back Panel.

Row 13 [13, 17, 17]: Rep row 29 of Back Panel, fasten off size small only.

Row [14, 18, 18] (sizes medium, large & X-large only): Ch 2, hdc in each st across, fasten off medium and large only.

Row [19] (X-large only): Ch 2, hdc in each st to end, fasten off.

Edging
Rep edging for Back Panel. *(14 [16, 20, 22] sc)*

Shoulder & Side Seams

Matching up sts of Front Panel with Back Panel with tapestry needle, sew 9 [11, 11, 13] sts at outside edge tog leaving 5 [5, 9, 9] sts at inside open for collar. Rep Shoulder Seam on opposite edge of Back Panel and 2nd Front Panel.

Matching up sts of bottom of Front Panel with Back Panel, with tapestry needle, sew 15 sts tog leaving 15 sts on each side unworked for sleeve.

Collar

Row 1: Join ocean with sc in first unworked st at neck edge of first Front Panel, sc in next 4 [4, 8, 8] sts, sc in each st across Back Panel, sc in each st on 2nd Front Panel, turn. *(22 [22, 30, 30] sc)*

Row 2: Ch 2, hdc in each st to end, fasten off.

Sleeve
Make 2.

Row 1: With ocean, ch 37 [37, 39, 39], dclp in 3rd ch from hook, dclp in each rem ch across.

Rows 2–17: Rep rows 2–5 of Back Panel consecutively.

Rows 18–20: Rep rows 2–4. At the end of last rep, leaving a long length for sewing, fasten off. With RS tog, matching sts of last row with bottom lps of row 1, sew seam tog.

Edging

Working in odd numbered row ends, join ocean with sc in any row, 2 sc in same row, 3 sc in next odd numbered row and each odd numbered row to end, join in beg sc, leaving a length for sewing, fasten off. *(30 sc)*

Matching sts with sts at armhole, with tapestry needle, attach sleeve.

Cuff

Rnd 1: Working in row ends at bottom of Sleeve, rep Edging for first end of sleeve, do not fasten off.

Rnd 2: Ch 2, hdc in each st to end, join in sl st in 2nd ch of beg ch-2, fasten off. *(30 hdc)*

Bottom Beaded Edging

Row 1 (sizes small & X-large only): Using a sewing needle, string beads into crochet cotton, working in sts along bottom, holding crochet cotton and ocean tog, attach with sc in first st, [ch 5, draw up a bead, ch 5, sk next 2 sts, sc in next st] across, fasten off. *(20 [28] sc)*

Row 1 (size medium only): With sewing needle, string beads onto crochet cotton, working in sts along bottom, holding crochet cotton and ocean tog, attach with sc in first st, ch 5, draw up a bead, ch 5, sk next 3 sts, sc in next st, [ch 5, draw up a bead, ch 5, sk next 2 sts, sc in next st] 19 times, ch 5, draw up a bead, ch 5, sk next 3 sts, sc in last st, fasten off. *(22 sc)*

Row 1 (size large only): With sewing needle, string beads onto crochet cotton, working in sts along bottom, holding crochet cotton and ocean tog, attach with sc in first st, ch 5, draw up a bead, ch 5, sk next 3 sts, sc in next st, [ch 5, draw up a bead, ch 5, sk next 2 sts, sc in next st] across to end, fasten off. *(25 sc)* ♣

BLUE FLASH SHAWL CONTINUED FROM PAGE 74

Special Stitches

3-double crochet cluster (3-dc cl): [Yo, insert hook in next ch-1 sp, yo, draw up a lp] 3 times, yo, draw through all 7 lps on hook, ch 1 to lock.

Shawl

Row 1: Ch 46, sc in 2nd ch from hook, sc in each rem ch across, turn. *(45 sc)*

Row 2: Ch 3 *(counts as first dc)*, dc in each st across, turn.

Row 3: Ch 4 *(counts as first dc, ch-1)*, sk next st, dc in next st, [ch 1, sk next st, dc in next st] across, turn. *(23 dc; 22 ch-1 sps)*

Row 4: Ch 3, [**3-dc cl** *(see Special Stitch)* in next ch-1 sp, dc in next st] across, turn. *(23 dc; 22 cls)*

Row 5: Rep row 3.

Row 6: Ch 3, [dc in next ch-1 sp, dc in next st] across, turn.

Rows 7–66: Rep rows 3–6 consecutively.

Row 67: Ch 1, sc in each st across, fasten off.

Edging

Row 1: Working in ends of rows on long side, attach yarn with sl st in first row, ch 3, 2 dc in each end of each row to last row, dc in last row, fasten off. Rep row 1 of Edging on opposite long edge of shawl.

Fringe

Cut 3 lengths of yarn each 16 inches long, fold strands in half, insert hook in st on end of shawl, draw strands through at fold to form a lp on hook, draw cut ends through lp on hook, pull gently to secure. Rep Fringe in each st on each end of Shawl, trim ends even. ♣

CRAYON COLORS TOTE CONTINUED FROM PAGE 76

Rnd 21: Sc in each sc around.

Rnd 22: [Sc in each of next 7 sc, sk next sc] around, sl st to join in beg sc. *(56 sc)*

Rnd 23: Ch 1, working from right to left, work **reverse sc** *(see Illustration)* in each sc around, join in beg sc, fasten off.

Reverse Single Crochet

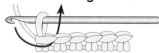

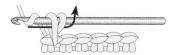

Strap

Row 1: With cherry, ch 225, sc in 2nd ch from hook, sc in each rem ch across, fasten off. *(224 sc)*

Row 2: Working in opposite side of foundation ch of row 1, attach wow, ch 1, hdc in same st as beg ch-1, [sk next ch, hdc in next ch, hdc in sk ch] across, ending with hdc in last ch, fasten off.

Row 3: Attach cherry in first hdc of row 2, ch 1, sc in same hdc as beg ch-1, sc in each hdc across.

Row 4: Holding ends of rows tog, matching sts and working through both thicknesses, sl st ends tog, fasten off.

Fold strap ring in half with ends facing top, with RS of Tote facing, place Tote between front and back of strap ring, align strap 3 inches from each side of Tote, making sure handles are even at top, pin in place, whipstitch strap to Tote. Sew buttons evenly sp down center front of tote using sections of wow where color matches buttons. ♣

FANCY FOOT WARMERS CONTINUED FROM PAGE 77

ring, ch 1, sc in each ch around, join in beg sc. *(24 sc)*

Rnd 2: Ch 1, sc in each sc around, join in beg sc, turn.

Rnds 3–22: Rep rnd 2.

Heel

Row 1: Ch 1, sc in each of next 12 sc, turn.

Rows 2 & 3: Rep row 1.

Row 4: Sl st into next sc, ch 1, sc in same sc as beg ch-1, sc in each sc across to last sc, leaving last sc unworked turn. *(10 sc)*

Rows 5 & 6: Rep row 4. At the end of row 6, fasten off. *(6 sc at end of row 6)*

Heel Shaping

Rnd 1: Place st markers in both corners next to tube top *(upper leg portion)* of sock and move as rnds progress, attach yarn at corner, ch 1, working in side edge of Heel rows work 6 sc, sc in each of next 6 sc of row 6 of Heel, work 6 sc across opposite side edge of Heel rows, sc in each rem 12 sc of row 2, join in beg sc, turn. *(30 sc)*

Rnds 2–4: Ch 1, sc around, **sc dec** *(see Stitch Guide)* at each corner st marker, join in beg sc, turn. *(24 sc)*

Rnds 5–15 [5–17]: Ch 1, sc in each sc around, join in beg sc, turn.

Toe Shaping

Rnd 1: Making sure heel is centered on bottom, place st markers evenly sp between 12 sts *(12 sts each top and bottom of sock)*, ch 1, *sc in each st to next st marker, sc dec in next 2 sts, rep from * around, join in beg sc, turn. *(22 sc)*

Rnd 2: Ch 1, *sc in each sc to next st marker, sc dec in next 2 sc, rep from * around, join in beg sc, turn. *(20 sc)*

Rnds 3–7: Rep rnd 2. *(10 sc)*

At the end of rnd 7, turn sock WS out and sl st top and bottom of Toe Shaping sts closed, fasten off, turn Sock RS out.

SHADES OF THE SOUTHWEST
CONTINUED FROM PAGE 81

Rnd 1 (RS): With size M hook, ch 3 (counts as first dc), dc evenly sp around outer edge of Panel, working (dc, ch 3, dc) in each corner, ending with (dc, ch 3) in same corner as beg ch-3, join in 3rd ch of beg ch-3, fasten off.

Rnd 2 (RS): Attach C with sl st in 2nd ch of corner ch-3 sp, ch 3, dc in next ch, *dc in each ch across to next corner, dc in first ch**, (dc, ch 2, dc) in 2nd ch, dc in 3rd ch, rep from * around, ending last rep at **, dc in same ch as beg ch-3, ch 2, join in 3rd ch of beg ch-3, fasten off.

Attaching Beads

Cut a 12-inch length of C, securely attach in area to be beaded *(use graph as a guide)*, attach beads where shown on graph by bringing needle up in position, thread bead on needle and draw yarn through, then bring needle down through panel. Be sure to cross over at least 1 strand of yarn on panel so that bead does not pull through to back side of panel. Four beads will be sewn on inside each diamond, weave in and secure rem length, rep for each diamond changing bead colors according to color sequence indicated on graph.

Assembly

With WS and bottom edges of 2 panels tog and

Border

Rnd 1 (RS): With size M hook, attach B with sl st in any corner, ch 3, 4 dc in same corner ch-2 sp, dc in each dc around, working 2 dc in each corner at top of joining of Panels and 5 dc in each of the rem 3 corners, join in 3rd ch of beg ch-3, fasten off.

Rnd 2 (RS): Attach B with sl st in 3rd dc of any 5-dc group of corner, ch 1, sc in same st as beg ch-1, *re-move lp from hook, insert size G hook through bead, pick up dropped lp and draw through bead, remove lp from hook, with size M pick up dropped lp, sk next dc, sc in each of next 3 dc, rep from * around alternating bead color, join in beg sc, fasten off. ✤

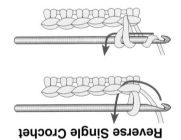

Reverse Single Crochet

working through both thicknesses, with size M hook, attach C, ch 1, **reverse sc** *(see illustration)* evenly sp across edge, fasten off. Rep until all 4 Afghan Panels are joined tog.

Trim

Rnd 1: Turn down rnds 1–9 of top of Sock to form a cuff, with size G hook attach 1 strand of yarn in rnd 1 of Sock, ch 1, sc in same ch as beg ch-1, ch 5, [sc in next ch, ch 5] around, join in beg sc, fasten off.

Rnd 2: With size G hook attach 1 strand of yarn

around vertical post of sc of rnd 1, ch 1, sc around **post** *(see Stitch Guide)* of same sc, ch 5, [sc around vertical post of next sc, ch 5] around, join in beg sc, fasten off.

Rnd 3: Rep rnd 2 around vertical post of sts of rnd 3 of Sock. ✤

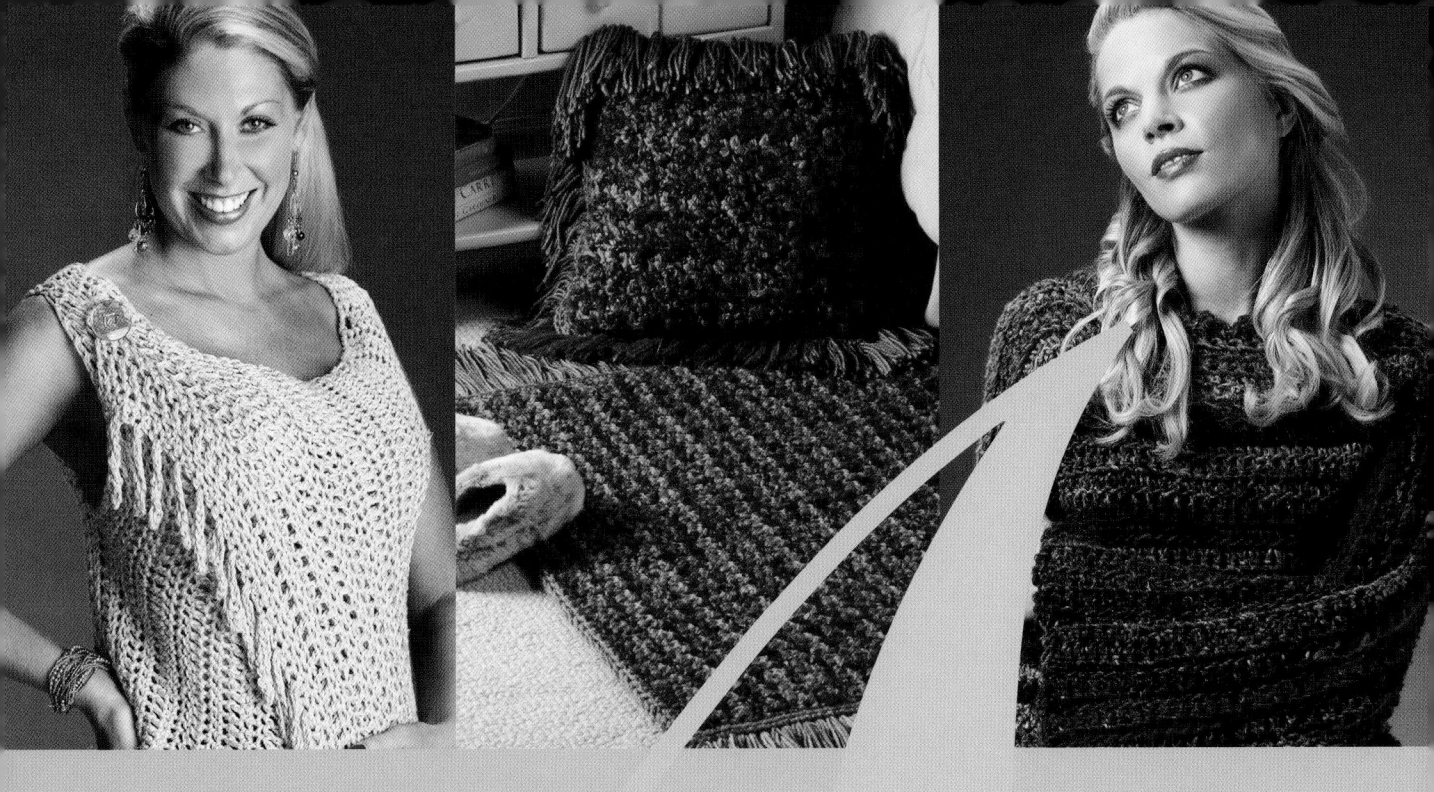

ALWAYS N-STYLE

Fashions and home accents that include traditional designs and classic patterns are always in vogue, whatever your wardrobe or decorating tastes may be. Updated colors and trendy yarns give fresh new appeal to this dazzling collection of popular styles.

COOL CROCHET CARDIGAN

Featuring the look of a wrap without the fuss, this light, silky-soft cardigan is the perfect little cover-up over a pretty strapless summer dress or skirt.

EASY

LIGHT 3

Finished Sizes

Small [medium, large/X-large, 2X-large]

Bust: 32-34 [36-38, 40-46, 48-50] inches

Finished Garment Measurements

Bust: 36 [40, 48, 52] inches

Materials

- Bernat Cool Crochet light (DK) sport weight yarn (1¾ oz/200 yds/50g per skein):
  summer cream
  7 [9, 11, 13] skeins #74008
- Size N/15/10mm crochet hook or size needed to obtain gauge
- Tapestry needle
- 2 stitch markers
- ⅞-inch beige button
- 1⅜-inch decorative button

Gauge

Rnds 1-3 = 3¼ inches; 9 dc of border = 3 inches

Pattern Notes

Weave in loose ends as work progresses.

Cardigan is crocheted vertically.

Right Front

Foundation row (WS): With 2 strands of soft beige held tog, ch 43 [46, 50, 55] sc in 2nd ch from hook, sc in each rem ch across, turn. (42 [45, 49, 54] sc)

Row 1: Ch 1, sc in each sc across, turn.

Row 2: Ch 3 (counts as first dc), dc in each sc across, turn.

Row 3: Ch 1, sc in each dc across, turn.

Rows 4-24 [4-30, 4-36, 4-42]: Rep rows 1-3 consecutively.

Right Armhole

Row 25 [31, 37, 43]: Ch 1, sc in each of next 19 [20, 21, 23] sc, ch 15 [17, 20, 23], sk next 15 [17, 20, 23] sc (armhole opening), sc in each of next 8 [8, 8, 8] sc, place a st marker in 4th sc of 8 [8, 8, 8] sc worked on top edge for placement of decorative button, turn.

Back

Row 26 [32, 38, 44]: Ch 3, dc in each of next 7 sc, 1 dc in each of next 15 [17, 20, 23] chs, dc in each of next 19 [20, 21, 23] sc, turn. (42 [45, 51, 54] dc)

Row 27 [33, 39, 45]: Ch 1, sc in each dc across, turn.

Rows 28-54 [34-66, 40-78, 46-90]: Rep rows 1-3.

Left Armhole

Row 55 [67, 79, 91]: Rep row 25 [31, 37, 42], placing 2nd st marker for smaller button.

Left Front

Row 56 [68, 80, 92]: Rep row 26 [32, 38, 44].

Rows 57–80 [69–98, 81–116, 93–134]: Rep rows 1–3.

Row 81 [99, 117, 135]: Ch 1, sc in each st across, turn.

Row 82 [100, 118, 136]: Ch 1, sc in first sc, [sc in each of next 2 sc, ch 18, sl st in first ch of ch-18] across, ending with sc in last sc, fasten off.

Finishing

Attach decorative 1⅜-inch button to row 25 [31, 37, 43] of Right Armhole at st marker. Use natural sps between dc sts for buttonhole.

Attach ⅞-inch button to row 55 [67, 79, 91] of Left Armhole at st marker. Use natural sps between dc sts for buttonhole. ❖

DESIGN BY LAURA GEBHARDT

FIREWORKS JACKET

Crochet a dynamite jacket stitched in plush, super bulky chenille yarn shot through with flashes of fiery colors. It's sure to spark up your wardrobe!

INTERMEDIATE

SUPER BULKY

Finished Sizes

Small [medium, large, X-large, 2X-large]

Bust: 32–34 [36–38, 40–42, 44–46, 48–50] inches

Finished Garment Measurements

Bust: 37½ [40, 45, 50, 55] inches

Materials

• Lion Brand Chenille Thick & Quick Prints super bulky (super chunky) weight yarn (75 yds/68m per skein):
    8 [9, 9, 10, 12] skeins #203 kaleidoscope print
• Size N/15/10mm crochet hook or size needed to obtain gauge
• Tapestry needle

Gauge

8 sts = 5 inches; 6 rows = 4 inches

Pattern Notes

Weave in loose ends as work progresses.
Join rounds with a slip stitch unless otherwise stated.

Back

Row 1: Ch 31 [33, 37, 41, 45] sc in 2nd ch from hook, dc in next ch, [sc in next ch, dc in next ch] across, turn. *(30 [32, 36, 40, 44] sts)*

Note: Row 2 of Back establishes pattern.
Row 2: Ch 1, sc in each dc, dc in each sc across, turn.
Rows 3–23 [3–25, 3–25, 3–27, 3–27]: Rep row 2.

Armhole Shaping

Row 24 [26, 26, 28, 28]: Sl st in each of first 3 [3, 5, 5, 7] sts, rep row 2 across to last 4 [4, 6, 6, 8] sts, **sc dec** *(see Stitch Guide)* in next 2 sts leaving rem sts unworked, turn. *(24 [26, 26, 30, 30] sts)*
Row 25 [27, 27, 29, 29]: Ch 3, sc in each dc, dc in each sc across, turn.
Row 26 [28, 28, 30, 30]: Ch 1, sk first st, sc in next st, work row 2 across to last 2 sts, sc dec in next 2 sts, turn. *(22 [24, 24, 28, 28] sts)*
Row 27–36 [29–38, 29–40, 31–44, 31–44]: Rep row 2 across row, turn. At the end of last row, fasten off.

Left Front

Row 1: Ch 17 [17, 19, 21, 25] sc in 2nd ch from hook, dc in next ch, [sc in next ch, dc in next ch] across, turn. *(16 [16, 18, 20, 24] sts)*
Rows 2–23 [2–25, 2–25, 2–27, 2–27]: Rep row 2 of Back.

Armhole Shaping

Row 24 [26, 26, 28, 28]: Work row 2 in pattern to

last 4 [4, 6, 6, 8] sts, sc dec in next 2 sts, leaving rem sts unworked, turn. *(13 [13, 13, 15, 17] sts)*

Row 25 [27, 27, 29, 29]: Ch 3, sc in each dc, dc in each sc across, turn.

Row 26 [28, 28, 30, 30]: Work row 2 in pattern to last 2 sts, **dc dec** *(see Stitch Guide)* in next 2 sts, turn. *(12 [12, 12, 14, 16] sts)*

Rows 27–32 [29–34, 29–36, 31–40, 31–40]: Pattern across row, turn.

Neck Shaping

Row 33 [35, 37, 41, 41]: Ch 1, pattern across first 6 [6, 6, 8, 8] sts, sc dec in next 2 sts. *(7 [7, 7, 9, 9] sts)*

Row 34 [36, 38, 42, 42]: Ch 3, pat across row, turn.

Row 35 [37, 39, 43, 43]: Ch 1, work row 2 in pattern across row to last 2 sts, sc dec in next 2 sts, turn. *(6 [6, 6, 8, 8] sts)*

Row 36 [38, 40, 44, 44]: Work row 2 in pattern across row, fasten off.

Right Front

Rows 1–23 [1–25, 1–25, 1–27, 1–27]: Rep rows 1–23 [1–25, 1–25, 1–27, 1–27] of Left Front.

Armhole Shaping

Row 24 [26, 26, 28, 28]: Sl st in first 3 [3, 5, 5, 7] sts, ch 1, work row 2 in pattern across row, turn. *(13 [13, 13, 15, 17] sts)*

Row 25 [27, 27, 29, 29]: Ch 1, pattern across row, turn.

Row 26 [28, 28, 30, 30]: Rep row 2 across row to last 2 sts, dc dec in next 2 sts, turn. *(12 [12, 12, 14, 16] sts)*

Rows 27–32 [29–34, 29–36, 31–40, 31–40]: Rep row 2 in pattern across row, turn.

Neck Shaping

Row 33 [35, 37, 41, 41]: Sl st in first 5 [5, 5, 7, 7] sts, ch 2 *(counts as a dec)*, rep row 2 in rem sts across, turn. *(7 [7, 7, 9, 9] sts)*

Row 34 [36, 38, 42, 42]: Work row 2 in pattern across row, turn.

Row 35 [37, 39, 43, 43]: Ch 2, dc in next st, pattern across row, turn. *(6 [6, 6, 8, 8] sts)*

CONTINUED ON PAGE 116

RAVISHING RUBY PULLOVER

Take it to town in style in a stunning sweater stitched in luscious super bulky yarn in a rich, multi-mix ruby. This classic design looks great on most any size.

INTERMEDIATE

SUPER BULKY

Finished Sizes

Small [medium, large, X-large]

Bust: 32–34 [36–38, 40–42, 44–46] inches

Finished Garment Measurements

Bust: 37½ [40, 45, 48¾] inches

Gauge

8 sts = 5 inches; 4 rows = 3 inches

Pattern Notes

Weave in loose ends as work progresses.
Join rounds with a slip stitch unless otherwise stated.

Special Stitches

Extended single crochet (extented sc): Insert hook in indicated st, yo, draw lp through, yo, draw through 1 lp on hook, yo, draw through 2 lps on hook.

Extended single crochet decrease (extented sc dec): [Insert hook in next st, yo, draw up a lp, yo,

Materials

- Red Heart Light & Lofty super bulky (super chunky) weight yarn (4½ oz/110yds/127g per skein):
    6 [6, 8, 9] skeins #9937 red grape multi
- Size N/15/10mm crochet hook or size needed to obtain gauge
- Tapestry needle

draw through 1 lp on hook] twice, yo, draw through all 3 lps on hook.

Back

Row 1: Ch 31 [33, 37, 40], **extented sc** (*see Special Stitches*) in 3rd ch from hook, extended sc in each rem ch across, turn. *(30 [32, 36, 39] sts)*

Row 2: Ch 2, extended sc in each extended sc across, turn.

Rows 3–6 [3–6, 3–8, 3–10]: Rep row 2.

Row 7 [7, 9, 11]: Ch 1 *(counts as beg dec)*, extended sc in each st across to last 2 extended sc, **esc dec** (*see Special Stitches*) in next 2 sts, turn. *(28 [30, 34, 37] sts)*

Row 8 [8, 10, 12]: Rep row 2.

Rows 9 & 10 [9 & 10, 11 & 12, 12 & 13]: Rep rows 7 and 8 [7 and 8, 9 and 10, 11 and 12]. *(26 [28, 32, 35] sts)*

Rows 11 & 12 [11 & 12, 13 & 14, 14 & 15]: Rep row 2.

Row 13 [13, 15, 17]: Ch 2, extended sc in same st as beg ch-2, extended sc in each st across to last extended sc, 2 extended sc in last esc, turn. *(28 [30, 34, 37] sts)*

Row 14 [14, 16, 18]: Rep row 2.

Rows 15 & 16 [15 & 16, 17 & 18, 19 & 20]: Rep rows 13 and 14 [13 and 14, 15 and 16, 17 and 18]. *(30 [32, 36, 39] sts)*

Rows 17 & 18 [17 & 18, 19–21, 21–23]: Rep row 2.

CONTINUED ON PAGE 116

DAZZLING JADE JACKET

With its classic Chanel styling and luxuriously soft high-fashion yarn, this go-anywhere jacket is perfect for any occasion from the bistro to the ballet.

EASY

5 BULKY

Finished Sizes

Small [medium, large, X-large]

Bust: 32–34 [36–38, 40–42, 44–46] inches

Finished Garment Measurements

Bust: 30 [34¾, 38¾, 42¾] inches

Gauge

10 sc = 4 inches; 12 rows = 4 inches

Pattern Notes

Weave in loose ends as work progresses.
Join rounds with a slip stitch unless otherwise stated.

Body

Row 1: Starting at bottom of Body, ch 76 [88, 100, 112] sc in 2nd ch from hook, sc in each rem ch across, turn. *(75 [87, 99, 111] sc)*

Row 2: Ch 1, sc in first st, [ch 1, sk next st, sc in next

Materials

- Moda Dea Outrageous bulky (chunky) weight eyelash yarn (1¾ oz/77 yds/50g per skein):
  9 [12, 12, 14] skeins #9523 aqua man
- Size N/15/10mm crochet hook or size needed to obtain gauge
- Tapestry needle

st] across, turn. *(38 [44, 50, 56] sc; 37 [43, 49, 55] ch-1 sps)*

Row 3: Ch 1, sc in first st, [sc in next ch-1 sp, sc in next sc] across, turn. *(75 [87, 99, 111] sc)*

Rows 4–25: Rep rows 2 and 3 alternately.

Row 26: Rep row 2.

First Front Panel

Row 1: Ch 1, sc in first st, [sc in next ch-1 sp, sc in next sc] 9 [11, 13, 15] times, turn. *(19 [23, 27, 31] sc)*

Row 2: Ch 1, sc in first st, [ch 1, sk next st, sc in next st] across, turn. *(10 [12, 14, 16] sc; 9 [11, 13, 15] ch-1 sps)*

Row 3: Ch 1, sc in first st, [sc in next ch-1 sp, sc in next sc] across, turn.

Rows 4–21 [4–25, 4–29, 4–33]: Rep rows 2 and 3. At the end of last rep, fasten off.

Back

Row 1: Sk next ch-1 sp on row 26 of Body, join yarn with sc in next st, [sc in next ch-1 sp, sc in next st] 17 [19, 21, 23] times, turn. *(35 [39, 43, 47] sc)*

Rows 2–21 [2–25, 2–29, 2–33]: Rep rows 2 and 3 of First Front Panel. At the end of last rep, fasten off.

2nd Front Panel

Row 1: Sk next ch-1 sp on row 26 of Body, join yarn with sc in next st, [sc in next ch-1 sp, sc in next st] 9

[11, 13, 15] times, turn. *(19 [23, 277, 31] sc)*

Rows 2–21 [2–25, 2–29, 2–33]: Rep rows 2 and 3 of First Front Panel. At the end of last rep, fasten off.

Joining Shoulders

Fold Front Panel over Back and working in sts at outside edge, with tapestry needle whipstitch 10 [14, 16, 18] sts tog leaving 9 [9, 11, 13] sts unworked. Rep whipstitch of sts on 2nd Front Panel and Back.

Edging

Row 1 (RS): Working in ends of rows, attach yarn at bottom edge of front, ch 1, work 127 [131, 143, 155] sc evenly sp up front, around back neck and down opposite front, turn.

Sleeve

Make 2.

Rnd 1 (small size only): Attach yarn with sc in sk ch-1 sp of row 26 of Body, sc in same sp, working in row ends, sc in each row around, join in beg sc, turn. *(44 sc)*

Rnd 1 (medium size only): Attach yarn with sc in sk ch-1 sp of row 26 of Body, working in row ends, [**sc dec** *(see Stitch Guide)* in next 2 rows] twice, sc in each row up to last 2 rows, sc dec in next 2 rows, join in beg sc, turn. *[48 sc]*

Rnd 1 (large size only): Attach yarn with sc in sk ch-1 sp of row 26 of Body, working in row ends, [sc dec in next 2 rows] twice, sc in each of next 9 rows, sc dec in next 2 rows] around, join in beg sc, turn. *[52 sc]*

Rnd 1 (X-large size only): Attach yarn with sc in sk ch-1 sp of row 26 of Body, working in row ends, [sc dec in next 2 rows] twice, [sc in each of next 5 rows, sc dec in next 2 rows] 8 times, sc in each of next 4 rows, sc dec in next 2 rows, join in beg sc, turn. *[52 sc]*

Rnd 2: Ch 1, sc in first st, ch 1, sk next st, [sc in next st, ch 1, sk next st] around, join in beg sc, turn. *(22 [24, 26, 28] sc; 22 [24, 26, 28] ch-1 sps)*

Row 3: Ch 1, sc in each sc and each ch-1 sp around, join in beg sc, turn.

Rnds 4–73: Rep rnds 2 and 3 alternately. At the end of row 73, fasten off. ❖

A WHIZ OF A SWEATER

The name says it all in the quick, easy style of this pullover that can be made in a day with big stitches and simple shaping. It's the perfect dress-up or dress-down sweater for any great look!

Finished Sizes

Small [medium, large]

Materials

• Noro Iro wool/silk bulky (chunky) weight yarn (3½ oz/130 yds/100g per skein):

   5 [5, 6] skeins #43 dark purples, greens, blacks

• Size N/15/10mm crochet hook or size needed to obtain gauge

• Tapestry needle

• Stitch Marker

Gauge

11 sts = 5 inches; 9 rows = 5 inches

Pattern Notes

Weave in loose ends as work progresses.
Join rounds with a slip stitch unless otherwise stated.

Sleeve Back

Row 1 (WS): Starting at neck edge, ch 104 [111, 119] sc in 2nd ch from hook, sc in each rem ch across, turn. *(103 [110, 118] sc)*

Row 2 (RS): Ch 1, working in **back lp** *(see Stitch Guide)* of each st, sc in each st across, turn.

Row 3: Ch 1, working in **front lp** *(see Stitch Guide)* of each st, sc in each st across, turn.

Rows 4–13 [4–15, 4–17]: Rep rows 2 and 3 alternately for a total of 13 [15, 17] rows. At the end of last rep, fasten off.

Sleeve Front

Row 1: Working on opposite side of foundation ch of row 1 of Sleeve Back, attach yarn in first ch, ch 1, sc in each of next 43 [45, 49] chs, ch 17 [20, 20], sk next 17 [20, 20] chs *(for neckline opening)*, sc in next 43 [45, 49] chs, turn.

Rows 2–13 [2–15, 2–17]: Rep rows 2–13 [2–15, 2–17] of Sleeve Back. At the end of last rep, do not fasten off.

Sleeve Seaming

Row 14 [16, 18]: At neck edge fold sleeves with RS tog, beg at cuff edge and working through both thicknesses of Sleeve Front and Back, ch 1, sc in each of next 33 [35, 37] sts, working in Sleeve Front only, sc in next 37 [40, 44] sts of front, sk 37 [40, 44] sts of Sleeve Back, holding rem sts of sleeve edges tog sc in each of next 33 [35, 37] sc sts of sleeve, fasten off.

Body

Rnd 1: With WS facing, working in each front lp across Sleeve Back, attach yarn with sc in first st, place a st marker in first st, sc in each rem st across Sleeve Back, continue in front lp of each st across Sleeve Front, do not join in beg sc. *(74 [80, 88] sc)*

Rnd 2 (WS): Move st marker as work progresses, working in front lp of each st, sc in each st around, do not join. *(74 [80, 88] sc)*

Rep rnd 2 until Body measures 20 [21, 22] inches or to desired length, sl st in next st, turn.

Body Trim

Rnd 1: With RS facing, ch 1, sc in same st as beg ch-1, sc in next sc, ch 3, sl st in top of 2nd sc, [sc in each of next 2 sc, ch 3, sl st in top of 2nd sc] around, join in beg sc, fasten off.

Neckline Trim

Rnd 1: With RS facing, attach yarn at back neck, ch 1, sc in same st as beg ch-1, sc in next st, ch 3, sl st in top of 2nd sc, [sc in each of next 2 sts, ch 3, sl st in top of 2nd sc] around, join in beg sc, fasten off. ❖

RAGGEDY STRIPES

Colorful novelty yarn that looks like tiny bits of torn fabric creates the bright, bodacious stripes in this vivid turquoise blue jacket accented with big wood buttons.

INTERMEDIATE

Finished Sizes
Small [medium, large]
Bust: 37 [40, 43] inches

Gauge
Size N hook: 8 sc or 8 dc = 4 inches; 10 rows = 4 inches

Pattern Notes
Weave in loose ends as work progresses.

6 SUPER BULKY

5 BULKY

Materials
- Tahki Baby wool super bulky (super chunky) weight yarn (60 yds/100g per ball):
  - 10 [11, 12] balls #39 turquoise *(MC)*
- Tahki Poppy ribbon bulky (chunky) weight yarn (1¾ oz/81 yds/50g per skein):
  - 5 [5, 6] skeins #09 yellow/pink *(CC)*
- Sizes K/10½/6.5mm and N/15/10mm crochet hooks or size needed to obtain gauge
- Tapestry needle
- 38mm wooden buttons: 5
- 8-inch square cardboard

Join rounds with a slip stitch unless otherwise stated. When changing yarn color, do not fasten off, carry up side edge of piece.

Back
Foundation row: With size N hook and MC, ch 31 [34, 37], sc in 2nd ch from hook, sc in each rem ch across, turn. *(30 [33, 36] sc)*

Row 1 (RS): Ch 1 *(counts as first st)*, sk first st, sc in each rem st across, turn. *(30 [33, 36] sc)*

Row 2: Change color *(see Stitch Guide)* to CC, ch 4 *(counts as first dc, ch-1),* *dc in each of next 2 sc, ch 1, sk 1 st, rep from * 8 [9, 10] times, ending with dc in top of end st, turn.

Row 3: Ch 1 *(does not count as first sc)*, sc in first dc, sc in next ch-1 sp, *sc in each of next 2 dc, sc in next ch-1 sp, rep from * across, ending with sc in 3rd ch of beg ch-4, turn. *(30 [33, 36] sc)*

Row 4: Change color to MC, ch 1, sk first st, dc in sk st 2 rows below, *sc in each of next 2 dc, 1 dc in the sk st 2 rows below, rep from * across, ending with sc in last st, turn.

Row 5: Ch 1, sk first st, sc in each st across, turn. Rep rows 2–5 until Back measures 12½ [13, 13½] inches from beg, ending with row 4 and CC.

Armhole Shaping

Sl st in 3 sts, working pattern of row 5, work sc in each st to last 3 sts, leaving last 3 sts unworked, turn. *(24 [27, 30] sc)*

Attach CC, beg with row 2, in established pattern of rows 2–5 until armhole measures 8½ [9, 9½] inches, fasten off.

Left Front

Foundation row: With size N hook and MC, ch 16 [19, 22] sc in 2nd ch from hook, sc in each rem ch across, turn. *(15 [18, 21] sc)*

Work Left Front the same as Back until the same length as Back to armhole, ending with row 4.

Armhole Shaping

Sl st over 3 sts, working pattern of row 5, work sc in each st across row, turn. *(12 [15, 18] sc)*

Attach CC, beg with row 2, work in established pattern of rows 2–5 until armhole measures 7 [8, 8½] inches, ending with row 3 at armhole edge, turn.

Neck Shaping

Rep row 4 across next 6 [9, 12] sts leaving last 6 [6, 6] sts unworked, turn, fasten off and rejoin CC, continue in established pat on rem 6 [9, 12] sts until Left Front measures the same as Back, fasten off.

Right Front

Foundation Row: With size N hook and MC, ch 16 [19, 22] sc in 2nd ch from hook, sc in each rem ch across, turn. *(15 [18, 21] sc)*

Work Right Front the same as Back until the same length as Back to armhole, ending with row 4.

Armhole Shaping

Working row 5 of pattern, work across 12 [15, 18] sts, turn. *(12 [15, 18] sc)*

Attach CC, beg with row 2 in established pat of rows 2–5 until armhole measures 7 [8, 8½] inches, ending with row 3 neckline edge, turn.

Neck Shaping

Sl st in each of next 6 [6, 6] sts, work row 4 across next 6 [9, 12] sts, turn, continue in established pat on rem 6 [9, 12] sts until Right Front measures the same as Back, fasten off.

Sleeve

Make 2.

Foundation row: With size K hook and MC, ch 19 [19, 19], sc in 2nd ch from hook, sc in each rem ch across, turn. *(18 [18, 18] sc)*

Rows 1–5: Rep rows 1–5 of Back. At the end of row 5, change to size N hook.

Rows 6–13: Rep rows 2–5 of Back.

Rows 14–16: Rep rows 2–4 of Back.

Row 17: Rep row 5 of Back, inc 1 sc at each beg and end of row. *(20 [20, 20] sc)*

Row 18: Ch 3, dc in next st, [ch 1, sk 1 st, dc in each of next 2 sts] 6 times, turn. *(14 dc; 6 ch-1 sps)*

Row 19: Ch 1, sc in each of next 2 dc, [sc in next ch-1 sp, sc in each of next 2 dc] across, turn.

Row 20: Ch 1, sk first sc, sc in 2nd st, dc in sk st 2 rows below, sc in each of next 2 sts, [dc in sk st 2 rows below, sc in each of next 2 sts] across, turn.

Row 21: Ch 1, sk first st, sc in each rem st across, turn.

Rows 22–29: Rep rows 2–5 of Back.

Rows 30–32: Rep rows 2–4 of Back.

Row 33: Rep row 17 of Sleeve. *(22 [22, 22] sc)*

Continue to work as established on 22 [22, 22] sts until Sleeve measures 16 inches from beg.

For large size only: Inc 1 st at beg and end of next row. *(22 [22, 24] sts)*

Continue to work as established until Sleeve measures 17 [17, 17½] inches from beg, ending with row 4 pat of Back.

Sleeve Cap Shaping

Row 1: Sl st in each of next 3 sts, rep row 5 of back across to last 3 sts, leaving last 3 sts unworked, turn. *(16 [16, 18] sts)*

Work rows 2–5 of Back until Cap Shaping measures 6 [6½, 6½] inches, ending with a row 3 of pat, change to size K hook. Rep rows 4 and 5, then fasten off sizes small and medium only. For large size only, with MC work 1 row of sc, fasten off.

CONTINUED ON PAGE 117

DESIGN BY KATHERINE ENG

KALEIDOSCOPE COLORS CLOCHE

A delicious mix of cotton and fashion yarns in festive colors gives fun appeal to this trendy hat. Natural wood beads add a polished finishing touch.

Finished Size
Adult

Materials
- TLC Cotton Plus medium (worsted) weight yarn (3½ oz/186 yds/100g per skein):
  1 skein #3503 spruce
- Moda Dea Swirl bulky (chunky) weight yarn (1¾ oz/62 yds/50g per skein):
  1 skein #3945 carnival
- Sizes H/8/5mm and N/15/10mm crochet hooks or size needed to obtain gauge
- Tapestry needle
- 8mm natural wood bead
- 20mm tear drop natural wood beads: 2

Gauge
Size N hook: Rnds 1 & 2 = 3 inches

Pattern Notes
Weave in loose ends as work progresses.

Join rounds with a slip stitch unless otherwise stated. Work with 1 strand each color held together throughout.

Cloche
Rnd 1: With size N hook, holding one strand each spruce and carnival, ch 4, sl st to join to form a ring, ch 1, [sc in ring, ch 3] 8 times, join in beg sc. *(8 ch-3 sps)*

Rnd 2: Sl st into next ch-3 sp, ch 1, sc in same ch sp as beg ch-1, ch 3, [sc in next ch-3 sp, ch 3] around, join in beg sc.

Rnd 3: Ch 1, sc in same sc as beg ch-1, *ch 3, sc in next ch-3 sp, ch 3**, sc in next sc, rep from * around, ending last rep at **, join in beg sc. *(16 ch-3 sps)*

Rnds 4–10: Rep rnd 2.

Rnd 11: Ch 1, sc in same sc as beg ch-1, *ch 1, sc in next ch-3 sp, ch 1**, sc in next sc, rep from * around, ending last rep at **, join in beg sc. *(32 ch-1 sps)*

Rnd 12: With size H hook, [ch 2, sk next ch-1 sp, sl st in next sc] around, join in same sc as beg ch-2, fasten off. *(32 ch-2 sps)*

CONTINUED ON PAGE 118

DIAMONDS ARE FOREVER

Sumptuous bulky weight nylon yarn gives lavish look and feel to this beautiful scarf and a pretty diamond pattern created with clusters gives it tempting texture.

EASY

5 BULKY

Finished Size

4¼ x 60 inches, excluding Fringe

Gauge

4 sc = 2 inches; 12 rows = 7 inches

Pattern Note

Weave in loose ends as work progresses.

Special Stitch

Cluster (cl): [Yo, insert hook in free lp of sc 2 rows below next sc, yo, draw up a lp] 3 times, yo, draw

Materials

• Patons Allure nylon bulky (chunky) weight yarn (1¾ oz/47 yds/50g per ball):
    3 balls #04128 aquamarine
• Size N/15/10mm crochet hook or size needed to obtain gauge
• Tapestry needle

through all 7 lps on hook, ch 1 to lock, and sk sc directly behind cluster.

Scarf

Row 1 (RS): Ch 10, sc in 2nd ch from hook, sc in each rem ch across, turn. *(9 sc)*

Row 2: Ch 1, working in **front lp** *(see Stitch Guide)* of each st, sc across, turn.

Row 3: Ch 1, sc in each sc across, turn.

Row 4: Rep row 2.

Row 5: Ch 1, sc in each of next 4 sc, **cl** *(see Special Stitch)* in next st 2 rows below, sc in each of next 4 sc, turn. *(8 sc; 1 cl)*

Row 6: Ch 1, sc in front lp only of each of next 4 sts, sk ch-1 locking st of cl, sc in top of cl, sc in front lp of each of next 4 sts, turn. *(9 sc)*

Row 7: Ch 1, sc in each of next 3 sc, [cl in next st 2 rows below, sc in next sc] twice, sc in each of next 2 sc, turn. *(7 sc; 2 cls)*

CONTINUED ON PAGE 118

BY GLENDA WINKLEMAN

RUSTIC RETREAT RUG

Reminiscent of an old-fashioned braided rug, this rustic design, made in easy-care cotton yarn, looks great whether in a country home or a mountain cabin.

INTERMEDIATE

Finished Size

27 x 36½ inches

5 BULKY

Materials

- Red Heart Casual Cot'n Blend bulky (chunky) weight yarn (4 oz/140 yds/113g per skein):
    - 3 skeins #3339 majestic
    - 2 skein each #3427 preppie, #3463 mushroom and #3872 Newport
- Size N/15/10mm crochet hook or size needed to obtain gauge
- Tapestry needle

Gauge

7 sts = 4 inches; 7 rows = 4 inches

Pattern Notes

Weave in loose ends as work progresses.
Join rounds with a slip stitch unless otherwise stated.
Roll preppie, mushroom and Newport into 3 separate balls each.

CONTINUED ON PAGE 118

LUMBERJACK THROW

The masculine look and feel of the bold red and black plaid design in this rustic throw evokes thoughts of the rugged woodsmen of the Pacific Northwest.

EASY

Finished Size

40 x 50 inches

Gauge

4 sc = 2 inches

6
SUPER BULKY

5
BULKY

Materials

- Lion Brand Wool-Ease Thick & Quick super bulky (super chunky) weight yarn (6 oz/106 yds per skein):
    4 skeins #153 black *(A)*
    3 skeins #138 cranberry *(B)*
- Lion Brand Jiffy Thick & Quick super bulky (super chunky) weight yarn (5 oz/84 yds/140g per skein):
    3 skeins #210 Ozarks *(C)*
- Lion Brand Fun Fur bulky (chunky) weight eyelash yarn (1¾ oz/60 yds/50g per skein):
    3 skeins #153 black *(D)*
- Size N/15/10mm crochet hook or size needed to obtain gauge
- Large-eye tapestry needle

Pattern Notes

Weave in loose ends as work progresses.
Join rounds with a slip stitch unless otherwise stated.
Do not fasten off color not in use, carry along side edge of rows until needed.

Strip

Make 15.

Row 1: With A, ch 5, sc in 2nd ch from hook, sc in each rem ch across, turn. *(4 sc)*

Row 2: Ch 1, sc in each of next 4 sc, turn.

Row 3: Rep row 2.

Row 4: Ch 1, sc in each sc across **change color** *(see Stitch Guide)* to C, do not fasten off A, turn.

Rows 5–11: Rep row 2.

Row 12: Rep row 2, change color to A.

Rows 13–15: Rep row 2.

Row 16: Rep row 2, change color to B.

Rows 17–23: Rep row 2.

Row 24: Rep row 2, change color to A.

Rows 25–27: Rep row 2.

Row 28: Rep row 2, change color to C.

Rows 29–35: Rep row 2.

Row 36: Rep row 2, change color to A.

Rows 37–39: Rep row 2.

Row 40: Rep row 2, change color to B.

Rows 41–47: Rep row 2.
Rows 48–95: Rep rows 24–47.
Row 96: Ch 1, sc in each sc across, fasten off yarns.

Assembly

Row 1: Holding 2 strips with WS tog matching row 1 of first strip with row 96 of the 2nd strip to create plaid, working through both thicknesses attach 1 strand each A and D in end st, ch 1, sc in same st as beg ch-1, work 95 sc across edge working over ends of yarns carried along the edge of strips, fasten off. *(96 sc)*

Row 2: Hold next strip to previously joined strips placing WS tog and row 1 of this strip to row 96 of previous strip to create plaid, working through both thicknesses attach 1 strand each A and D in end st, ch 1, sc in same st as beg ch-1, work 95 sc across edge working over ends of yarns carried along edge of strips, fasten off. *(96 sc)*

Rep row 2 until all 15 strips are joined tog.

Border

Rnd 1: With WS facing holding tog 1 strand each A and D, attach strands in any st, ch 1, sc in each st around outer edge working 3 sc in each corner st and working over ends of yarns carried along edge of strips, join in beg sc, fasten off. ✤

TWILIGHT STRIPES RUG & PILLOW

The soft purple and deep blue hues of a twilight sky give soothing appeal to this beautiful rug and pillow worked in a lightly textured stitch pattern.

EASY

Finished Sizes
Rug: 23¼ x 31 inches, excluding Fringe
Pillow: 14 inches square

SUPER BULKY

MEDIUM

Materials
- Red Heart Bright & Lofty super bulky (super chunky) weight yarn (4 oz/95 yds/113g per skein):
    4 skeins #9956 grape crush
- Caron Simply Soft Brites medium (worsted) weight yarn (3 oz/157 yds/85g per skein):
    6 skeins #9610 grape
    4 skeins #9606 berry blue
- Sizes K/10½/6.5mm and N/15/10mm crochet hooks or size needed to obtain gauge
- Tapestry needle
- 14-inch square pillow form

Gauge
Size N hook: 2 rows = 1¼ inches; 5 sts = 3 inches

Pattern Notes
Weave in loose ends as work progresses.

Join rounds with a slip stitch unless otherwise stated. Use 1 strand of grape crush throughout. When using grape or berry blue use 3 strands of same color held together.

RUG

Row 1 (RS): With size N hook and 1 strand grape crush, ch 56, sc in 2nd ch from hook, sc in each rem ch across, turn. *(55 sc)*

Row 2: Change color *(see Stitch Guide)* to 3 strands of grape, ch 1, sc in first st, [dc in next st, sc in next st] across, turn.

Row 3: Change color to 1 strand grape crush, ch 3 *(counts as first dc)*, [sc in next st, dc in next st] across, turn.

Row 4: Change color to 3 strands of berry blue, ch 1, sc in first st, [dc in next st, sc in next st] across, turn.

Row 5: Rep row 3.

Row 6: Rep row 2.

Row 7: Rep row 3.

Row 8: Rep row 4.

Rows 9–36: Rep rows 5–8 consecutively.

Row 37 (RS): With 1 strand grape crush, ch 1, sc in each st across, fasten off.

Side Trim

Row 1 (RS): With size N hook, attach 3 strands of grape

in first sc of row 37, ch 1, sc in each st across, turn.

Row 2: Sl st in each sc across, fasten off.

Row 3 (RS): Attach 3 strands of grape in opposite side of foundation ch, ch 1, sc in same ch as beg ch-1, sc in each ch across, turn.

Row 4: Sl st in each sc across, fasten off.

End Trim

Row 1 (WS): With size K hook, attach 1 strand each grape and berry blue and working in ends of rows, ch 1, work 55 sc across, turn. *(55 sc)*

Row 2: Ch 1, sc in each sc across, turn.

Row 3: Sl st in each st across, fasten off.
Rep rows 1–3 on opposite end of Rug.

Fringe

Cut 2 strands each 12 inches long of grape and berry blue. Holding all 4 strands tog, fold in half, with WS

of Rug facing, insert hook in first st, draw strands through at fold to form a lp on hook, draw cut ends through lp on hook, pull ends to tighten. Rep Fringe in each st across each end of Rug.

PILLOW
Side
Make 2.

Row 1 (RS): With size N hook and 1 strand grape crush, ch 24, sc in 2nd ch from hook, sc in each rem ch across, turn. *(23 sc)*

Rows 2–20: Rep rows 2–20 of Rug.

Row 21 (RS): With 1 strand grape crush, ch 1, sc in each st across, fasten off.

Edging

Rnd 22 (RS): With size N hook, attach 1 strand grape

CONTINUED ON PAGE 119

FRUIT STRIPES THROW

Big, bold stripes of bright, fruity colors create the pleasing, eye-catching pattern in this vibrant afghan that is sure to delight kids of any age.

EASY

SUPER BULKY

Finished Size

44 x 54 inches, including Fringe

Materials

- Simply Soft Quick super bulky (super chunky) weight yarn (3 oz/50 yds per skein):
  - 4 skeins each #001 white, #0011 soft pink, #0012 watermelon, #0013 limelight and #0014 grape
- Size N/15/10mm crochet hook or size needed to obtain gauge
- Tapestry needle

Gauge

3 shell rows = 2½ inches; 1 post st and 2 shells = 4 inches

Pattern Notes

Weave in loose ends as work progresses.
Join rounds with a slip stitch unless otherwise stated.

Special Stitch

Shell: (2 dc, ch 1, 2 dc) in indicated st or sp.

Throw

Row 1 (WS): With white, ch 96, dc in 4th ch from hook, *[sk next 2 chs, **shell** (see Special Stitch) in next ch] twice, sk next 2 chs, dc in next ch, rep from * 9 times, dc in each of last 2 chs, turn. (20 shells, 13 dc)

Row 2 (RS): Ch 3 (counts as first dc), **fpdc** (see Stitch Guide) around vertical post of next dc, [shell in ch-1 sp of each of next 2 shells, fpdc around vertical post of single dc] across, ending with dc in last dc, turn.

Row 3 (WS): Ch 3, **bpdc** (see Stitch Guide) around vertical post of next dc, [shell in ch-1 sp of each of next 2 shells, bpdc around vertical post of single dc] across, ending with dc in last dc, turn.

Row 4: With grape, rep row 2.

Row 5: Rep row 3.

Row 6: Rep row 2.

Row 7: With soft pink, rep row 3.

Row 8: Rep row 2.

Row 9: Rep row 3.

Row 10: With watermelon, rep row 2.

Row 11: Rep row 3.

Row 12: Rep row 2.

Row 13: With limelight, rep row 3.

Row 14: Rep row 2.

Row 15: Rep row 3.

Row 16: With white, rep row 2.

Row 17: Rep row 3.

Row 18: Rep row 2.

Row 19: With grape, rep row 3.

Row 20: Rep row 2.

Row 21: Rep row 3.

Row 22: With soft pink, rep row 2.

Row 23: Rep row 3.

Row 24: Rep row 2.

Row 25: With watermelon, rep row 3.

Row 26: Rep row 2.

Row 27: Rep row 3.

Row 28: With limelight, rep row 2.

Row 29: Rep row 3.

Row 30: Rep row 2.

Row 31: With white, rep row 3.

Row 32: Rep row 2.

Row 33: Rep row 3.

Rows 34–63: Rep rows 4–33.

Fringe

Working across row 63, fringe is worked in each ch-1 sp of each shell and in each post st across. Working across opposite side of foundation ch, fringe is worked in sp between dc sts of each shell and in bases of dc sts between shells and sps between each group of 2 shells. Alternating 1 strand each of soft pink, watermelon, limelight and grape with 1 strand of white for each fringe. Cut 2 strands each 12 inches long, fold strands in half, insert hook into indicated st, draw strands through at fold to form a lp on hook, draw cut ends through lp on hook, pull gently to secure. For a fluffy look, separate plies of fringe. Trim ends even. ❖

FIREWORKS JACKET CONTINUED FROM PAGE 97

Row 36 [38, 40, 44, 44]: Work row 2 in pattern across row, fasten off.

Sleeve
Make 2.
Rows 1–26 [1–26, 1–26,1–28, 1–28]: Ch 19 [19, 19, 21, 25], work as for Back on 18 [18, 18, 20, 24] sts, inc 1 st each end of 5th [5th, 3rd, 3rd, 3rd] row and every following 4th row to 26 [26, 30, 32, 34] sts, then continue row 2 of pat until 26 [26, 26, 28, 28] rows are completed. *(26 [26, 30, 32, 34] sts)*
Row 27 [27, 27, 29, 29]: Sl st in first 3 [3, 5, 5, 7] sts, ch 1, rep row 2 of pat across row to last 4 [4, 6, 6, 8] sts, sc dec in next 2 sts, leaving rem sts unworked, turn. *(20 [20, 20, 22, 20] sts)*
Row 28 [28, 28, 30, 30]: Rep row 2 of pat across row, turn.
Row 29 [29, 29, 31, 31]: Ch 1, sc dec in next 2 sts, rep row 2 of pat across row to last 2 sts, sc dec in last 2 sts, turn. *(18 [18, 18, 20, 18] sts)*

Rows 30–34 [30–34] (sizes small & medium only): Rep row 29 [29]. At the end of row 34 [34], fasten off. *(8 [8] sts)*
Row [30, 32, 32] (sizes large, X-large & 2X-large): Rep pat row 2 across row, turn.
Row [31, 33, 33]: Ch 1, sc dec in next 2 sts, rep pat row 2 across row to last 2 sts, sc dec in next 2 sts, turn. *([16, 18, 16] sts)*
Rows [32 & 33, 34–36, 34–36]: Rep rows [30 & 31, 32 & 33, 32 & 33]. *([14, 14, 12] sts)*
Rows [34–36, 37 & 38, 37 & 38]: Rep row [31, 33, 33]. At the end of last rep, fasten off. *([8, 10, 8] sts)*
Sew shoulder seams of Back and Fronts. Sew Sleeve into armhole opening and sew sleeve and side seams.

Edging
Row 1 (RS): Attach yarn with sl st at bottom right front, ch 1, sc evenly sp up right front, around neckline and down left front, fasten off. ❧

RAVISHING RUBY PULLOVER CONTINUED FROM PAGE 98

Armhole Shaping
Row 19 [19, 22, 24]: Sl st in each of next 2 [3, 4, 4] sts, ch 1, extended sc in next st, extended sc in each st across to last 3 [4, 5, 5] sts, extended sc dec in next 2 sts, turn leaving rem sts unworked. *(26 [26, 28, 31] sts)*
Row 20 [20, 23, 25]: Rep row 2.
Row 21 [21, 24, 26]: Rep row 7 [7, 9, 11]. *(24 [24, 26, 29] sts)*
Rows 22–27 [22–27, 25–31, 27–35]: Rep row 2.

Neck Shaping
Row 28 [28, 32, 36]: Ch 2, extended sc in each of next 4 [4, 5, 6] sts, extended sc dec in next 2 sts, fasten off, sk next 11 [11, 11, 12] sts, attach yarn in next st, ch 1, extended sc in next st, extended sc in each rem st across, fasten off.

Front
Rows 1–24 [1–24, 1–28, 1–30]: Rep rows 1–24 [1–24, 1–28, 1–30] of Back. *(24 [24, 26, 29] sts)*

Left Neck & Shoulder Shaping
Row 25 [25, 29, 31]: Ch 2, extended sc in each of next 5 [5, 6, 7] sts, extended sc dec in next 2 sts, turn. *(7 [7, 8, 9] sts)*
Row 26 [26, 30, 32]: Rep row 2.
Row 27 [27, 31, 33]: Ch 2, esc in each st across to last 2 sts, extended sc dec in next 2 sts, turn. *(6 [6, 7, 8] sts)*
Row 28 [28, 32, 34]: Rep row 2, fasten off.

Right Neck & Shoulder Shaping
Row 25 [25, 29, 31]: Sk next 8 [8, 8, 9] sts after Left Shoulder and attach yarn in next st, ch 1, each in

next st, extended sc in each rem st across, turn. *(7 [7, 8, 9] sts)*

Row 26 [26, 30, 32]: Rep row 2.

Row 27 [27, 31, 33]: Ch 1, extended sc in next st, extended sc in each rem st across, turn. *(6 [6, 7, 8] sts)*

Row 28 [28, 32, 34]: Rep row 2, fasten off.

Sleeve
Make 2.
Row 1–22 [1–22, 1–24, 1–24]: Ch 17 [17, 19, 19] and work as given for Back on 16 [16, 18, 18] sts inc 1 st each end of 5th [5th, 3rd, 3rd] row and every following 4th row to 24 [24, 28, 28] sts, then work rem rows even in esc across each row, turn.

Shaping Cap
Row 23 [23, 25, 25]: Sl st in each of next 2 [3, 4, 4] sts, extended sc in next st and in each st across to last 3 [4, 5, 5] sts, esc dec in next 2 sts, turn leaving rem sts unworked. *(18 [18, 20, 20] sts)*

Row 24 [24, 26, 26]: Rep row 2.

Row 25 [25, 27, 27]: Ch 1, extended sc in each st across to last 2 sts, extended sc dec in next 2 sts, turn. *(16 [16, 18, 18] sts)*

Rows 26–29 [26–29, 28–32, 28–33]: Rep row 25 [25, 27, 27]. At the end of last rep, fasten off. *(8 [8, 8, 6] sts)* Sew Front and Back tog at shoulders. Set in sleeves and sew sleeve and side seams.

Collar
Rnd 1 (RS): Attach yarn with sl st in first st after right shoulder seam, ch 1, sc in same st as beg ch-1, sc in each of next 11 [11, 11, 12] sts across back of neck, 6 [6, 6, 9] sc down left shoulder, 8 [8, 8, 9] sc across front neck and 6 [6, 6, 9] sts up right shoulder, join in beg sc. *(32 [32, 32, 40] sts)*

Rnd 2: Ch 3 *(counts as first dc)*, dc in each rem sc around, join in 3rd ch of beg ch-3.

Rnds 3–9 [3–9, 3–9, 3–11]: Ch 2, [**fpdc** *(see Stitch Guide)* around vertical post of next st, **bpdc** *(see Stitch Guide)* around vertical post of next st] around, join in 2nd ch of beg ch-2. At the end of last rep, fasten off. ✤

RAGGEDY STRIPES CONTINUED FROM PAGE 106

Assembly
Separate a length of MC into 2 plies, it will divide very easily and makes it much easier for sewing the garment. Matching sts, sew shoulder seams, sew each sleeve into armhole opening and sew side and sleeve seams.

Front & Neckline Border
Row 1 (RS): With size K hook, attach MC in bottom right front corner, making sure that border rem flat, ch 1, sc evenly sp up Right Front, working 3 sc in last st, sc evenly sp around neckline, 3 sc in first st of Left Front, sc evenly sp down Left Front, turn.

Row 2: Ch 1, sk first sc, sc in each sc across Left Front, work 3 sc in center corner sc, sc in each sc around neckline, 3 sc in center sc of Right Front, ch 2, sk 2 sts *(buttonhole)*, [sc in each of next 6 sc, ch 2, sk next 2 sc] 4 times, sc in each rem sc to end of row, turn.

Row 3: Ch 1, sk first sc, sc in each sc, 2 sc in each ch-2 sp up Right Front, 3 sc in center corner sc at neckline, sc around neckline, 3 sc in center corner sc, sc in each rem sc down Left Front, fasten off.

Separate a strand of MC into 2 plies; sew buttons to Left Front opposite buttonholes. ✤

ALWAYS N-STYLE **117**

KALEIDOSCOPE COLORS CLOCHE CONTINUED FROM PAGE 107

Tie

With size N hook, holding one strand of each spruce and carnival tog, leaving a 4-inch length at beg, ch 105, leaving a 4-inch length, fasten off.

Weave ch through ch-1 sps of rnd 11. Tie ends in a bow at side. Place a 20mm bead on each end of tie. Attach an 8-inch length of each color to end of each tie, fold ends and tie in an overhand knot, trim ends to 1½ inches.

Flower

Rnd 1: Rep rnd 1 of Cloche. *(8 ch-3 sps)*

Rnd 2: Working behind rnd 1 between sc sts, ch 1, sc between next 2 sc into ch-4 ring, [ch 4, sc into ring between next 2 sc of rnd 1] 7 times, ch 4, join in beg sc, leaving a length of yarn, fasten off. Sew 8mm bead to center of Flower. Position flower at side over bow and sew in place to Cloche. ❖

DIAMONDS ARE FOREVER CONTINUED FROM PAGE 108

Row 8: Ch 1, sc in front lp only of each sc, sc in top of each cl, turn. *(9 sc)*

Row 9: Ch 1, sc in each of next 2 sc, [cl in next sc 2 rows below, sc in next sc] twice, cl in next sc, sc in each of next 2 sc, turn. *(6 sc; 3 cl)*

Row 10: Rep row 8.

Row 11: Rep row 7.

Row 12: Rep row 8.

Row 13: Rep row 5.

Row 14: Rep row 8.

Row 15: Rep row 3.

Row 16: Rep row 2.

Rows 17–100: Rep rows 5–16 consecutively. At the end of last rep, fasten off.

Fringe

With RS facing, attach yarn with sl st in first st of last row of Scarf, [ch 25, sk next st, sl st in next st] 4 times, fasten off.

With RS facing attach yarn with sl st in first ch of opposite side of foundation ch of Scarf, [ch 25, sk next ch, sl st in next ch] 4 times, fasten off. ❖

RUSTIC RETREAT RUG CONTINUED FROM PAGE 109

Rug

Rnd 1 (RS): With 3 strands of mushroom, ch 15, 3 sc in 2nd ch from hook, sc in each of next 12 chs, 3 sc in last ch, working on opposite side of foundation ch, sc in each of next 12 chs, join in beg sc, fasten off. *(30 sc)*

Rnd 2: Join majestic in beg sc, ch 1, [2 sc in each of next 3 sc, sc in each of next 12 sc] twice, join in beg sc fasten off. *(36 sc)*

Rnd 3: Join preppie in beg sc, ch 1, sc in each of next 2 sc, 2 sc in each of next 2 sc, sc in each of next 16 sc, 2 sc in each of next 2 sc, sc in each of next 14 sc, join in beg sc, fasten off. *(40 sc)*

Rnd 4: Join Newport in beg sc, ch 1, sc in each of next 2 sc, 2 sc in each of next 4 sc, sc in each of next 16 sc, 2 sc in each of next 4 sc, sc in each of next 14 sc, join in beg sc, fasten off. *(48 sc)*

Rnd 5: Join mushroom in beg sc, ch 1, sc in each of next 2 sc, *2 sc in next sc, sc in next sc, 2 sc in next sc, sc in each of next 2 sc, 2 sc in next sc, sc in next sc, 2 sc in next sc*, sc in each of next 16 sc, rep bet *, sc in each of next 14 sc, join in beg sc, fasten off. *(56 sc)*

Rnd 6: Join majestic in beg sc, ch 1, sc in each of next 6 sc, [2 sc in next sc, sc in next sc] 3 times, sc in each of next 22 sc, [2 sc in next sc, sc in next sc] 3 times, sc in each of next 16 sc, join in beg sc, fasten off. *(62 sc)*

Rnd 7: Join preppie in beg sc, ch 1, sc in each sc around, join in beg sc, fasten off.

Rnd 8: Join Newport in beg sc, ch 1, sc in each of next 6 sc, *[2 sc in next sc, sc in next sc] 4 times*, sc in each of next 23 sc, rep bet *, sc in each of next 17 sc, join in beg sc, fasten off. *(70 sc)*

Rnd 9: Join mushroom in beg sc, ch 1, sc in each of next 5 sc, *[2 sc in next sc, sc in next sc] 8 times*, sc in each of next 19 sc, rep bet *, sc in each of next 14 sc, join in beg sc fasten off. *(86 sc)*

Rnd 10: Join majestic, rep rnd 7.

Rnd 11: Rep rnd 7.

Rnd 12: Join Newport, rep rnd 7.

Rnd 13: Join mushroom in beg sc, ch 1, sc in each of next 12 sc, *[2 sc in next sc, sc in each of next 2 sc] 5 times*, sc in each of next 28 sc, rep bet *, sc in each of next 16 sc, join in beg sc fasten off. *(96 sc)*

Rnd 14: Rep rnd 10.

Rnd 15: Rep rnd 7.

Rnd 16: Join Newport in beg sc, ch 1, sc in each of next 12 sc, *[2 sc in next sc, sc in next sc] 10 times*, sc in each of next 28 sc, rep bet *, sc in each of next 16 sc, join in beg sc fasten off. *(116 sc)*

Rnd 17: Join mushroom, rep rnd 7.

Rnd 18: Rep rnd 10.

Rnd 19: Join preppie in beg sc, ch 1, sc in each of next 12 sc, *[2 sc in next sc, sc in each of next 2 sc] 10 times*, sc in each of next 28 sc, rep bet *, sc in each of next 16 sc, join in beg sc fasten off. *(136 sc)*

Rnd 20: Rep rnd 12.

Rnd 21: Rep rnd 17.

Rnd 22: Rep rnd 10.

Rnd 23: Join mushroom in beg sc, ch 1, [sc in each of next 7 sc, 2 sc in next sc] around, join in beg sc, fasten off. *(153 sc)*

Rnd 24: Join majestic in beg sc, ch 1, [sc in each of next 2 sc, ch 3, sl st in last sc] around, join in beg sc, fasten off. ❧

TWILIGHT STRIPES RUG & PILLOW CONTINUED FROM PAGE 113

crush with sc in first st, sc in each of next 20 sts, 3 sc in last st, work 21 sc evenly sp across side edge, ending with 3 sc in last st, working in opposite side of foundation ch, sc in each of next 21 sts, 3 sc in last st, work 21 sc evenly sp across rem side edge, ending with 3 sc in last st, join in beg sc, fasten off. *(96 sc)*

Joining

Rnd 1: Holding WS of pillow pieces with tog and with size K hook, attach 1 strand each grape and ber-ry blue with sc in first st, adding sts as needed due to the use of a smaller hook, sc around 3 sides of pillow, working 3 sc in each center corner sc, insert pillow form and continue to sc across 4th side edge, join in beg sc, turn.

Rnd 2: Sl st in each st around, fasten off.

Fringe

Using 8-inch lengths of yarn, rep Fringe the same as for Rug on all 4 sides of the Pillow. ❧

P-HOOK
PIZZAZZ!

A variety of fanciful yarns in an assortment of colors, weights and fibers make it fun and easy to add pizzazz to almost any project. From glamorous fashions and accessories to eye-catching home accents, these projects are filled with plenty of panache!

BRANDYWINE CAPELET

Worked in a delicious mix of rich chestnut and cognac shades, this super-easy capelet is made using only a simple one-row repeat of single crochet stitches.

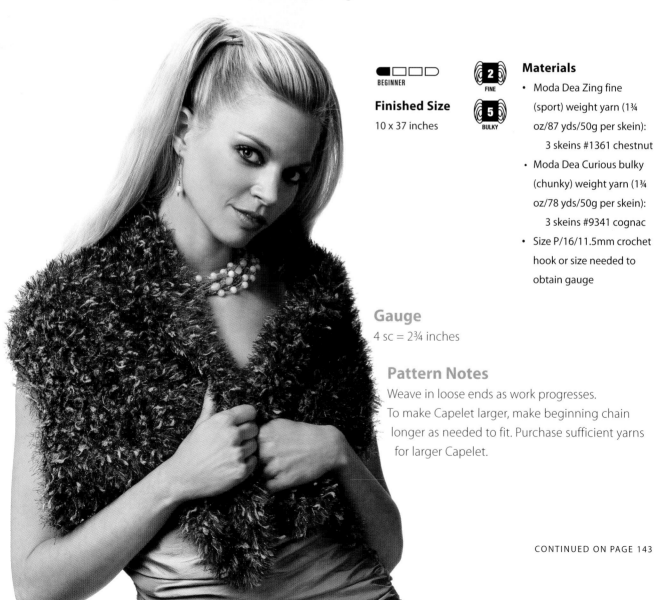

BEGINNER

Finished Size
10 x 37 inches

2 FINE

5 BULKY

Materials
- Moda Dea Zing fine (sport) weight yarn (1¾ oz/87 yds/50g per skein):
    3 skeins #1361 chestnut
- Moda Dea Curious bulky (chunky) weight yarn (1¾ oz/78 yds/50g per skein):
    3 skeins #9341 cognac
- Size P/16/11.5mm crochet hook or size needed to obtain gauge

Gauge
4 sc = 2¾ inches

Pattern Notes
Weave in loose ends as work progresses.
To make Capelet larger, make beginning chain longer as needed to fit. Purchase sufficient yarns for larger Capelet.

CONTINUED ON PAGE 143

DISCO DAZZLE

Punch up your winter wardrobe with these ultra-cool accessory set stitched in smooth, medium weight yarn punched up with luscious eyelash yarn with a flash of sparkle.

BEGINNER

4 MEDIUM

Finished Sizes

Scarf: 4 x 66 inches, excluding Fringe

Headband: 21 inches in diameter x 1 inch wide

5 BULKY

Materials

- Caron Simply Soft medium (worsted) weight yarn (2½ oz/131 yds/70.9g per skein):
    1 skein #2628 dark country blue
- Bernat Disco bulky (chunky) weight yarn (1¾ oz/71 yds/50g per skein):
    2 skeins #68110 boogie blue
- Size P/16/11.5mm crochet hook or size needed to obtain gauge
- Yarn needle

Gauge

7 sc = 4 inches; 4 rows = 4 inches

Pattern Notes

Weave in loose ends as work progresses.

Join rounds with a slip stitch unless otherwise stated.

Scarf

Row 1: Holding 1 strand each color tog, ch 8, sc in 2nd ch from hook, sc in each rem ch across, turn. *(7 sc)*

Row 2: Ch 3 *(counts as first dc)*, dc in each sc across, turn. *(7 dc)*

Row 3: Ch 1, sc in each dc across, turn. *(7 sc)*

Rep rows 2 and 3 alternately until Scarf measures 66 inches from beg, do not fasten off.

Fringe

Working across last row of Scarf, sl st in first st, [ch 20, sk next st, sl st in next st] 3 times, fasten off.

Working on opposite end of Scarf, holding 1 strand each color tog, attach with sl st in first ch of opposite

CONTINUED ON PAGE 143

BLUE LAGOON

The vivid aqua shades of a cool lagoon are beautifully blended in the multicolor mix of boucle and eyelash yarns in this flattering, easy-to-make swing coat.

EASY

4
MEDIUM

Finished Sizes

5
BULKY

Small [medium, large, X-large]
Bust: 32–34 [36–38, 40-42, 44–46] inches

Finished Garment Measurements

Bust: 40 [44, 46, 52] inches

Gauge

6 sts = 4 inches; 7 rows = 8 inches

Materials

- Lion Brand Boucle super bulky (super chunky) weight yarn (2½ oz/57 yds/52g per skein):
    14 [15, 17, 20] skeins #202 lime blue
- Lion Brand Fun Fur bulky (chunky) weight eyelash yarn (1¾ oz/60 yds/50g per skein):
    13 [14, 16, 19] skeins #148 turquoise
- 4-ply medium (worsted) weight yarn for seaming:
    20 yds blue
- Size P/16/11.5mm crochet hook or size needed to obtain gauge
- Yarn needle
- 1½-inch toggle or button

Pattern Notes

Weave in loose ends as work progresses.
Join rounds with a slip stitch unless otherwise stated.
Entire coat is worked holding 1 strand each lime blue and turquoise together.

Special Stitches

3-double crochet cluster (3-dc cl): (Yo, insert hook in indicated sp, yo, draw up a lp, yo, draw through 2 lps on hook) 3 times in same sp, yo, draw through all 4 lps on hook, ch 1 to lock.

Back

Row 1: With 1 strand each lime blue and turquoise held tog, ch 42 [45, 48, 51], dc in 4th ch from hook, dc in each rem ch across, turn. *(40 [43, 46, 49] dc)*
Row 2: Ch 3 *(counts as first dc)*, dc in each dc across, turn.
Rows 3 & 4: Rep row 2.
Row 5: Ch 2, dc in next dc *(counts as beg dc dec)*, dc in each dc across to last 2 sts, **dc dec** *(see Stitch Guide)* in next 2 sts, turn. *(38 [41, 44, 47] dc)*
Rows 6–21: Rep rows 2–5. *(30 [33, 36, 39] dc)*
Rows 22–26: Rep row 2.

Armhole Shaping
Row 27: Sl st in each of first 4 [4, 5, 5] sts, ch 3, dc in each st across to last 3 [3, 4, 4] sts, leaving rem sts unworked, turn. *(24 [27, 28, 31] dc)*
Rows 28–33 [28–33, 28–35, 28–35]: Rep row 2. At the end of last rep, fasten off.

Left Front
Row 1: With 1 strand each lime blue and turquoise held tog, ch 23 [25, 27, 29], dc in 4th ch from hook, dc in each rem ch across, turn. *(21 [23, 25, 27] dc)*
Row 2: Ch 3, dc in each dc across, turn.
Rows 3 & 4: Rep row 2.
Row 5: Ch 2, dc in next dc *(counts as beg dc dec)*, dc in each rem dc across, turn. *(20 [22, 24, 26] dc)*
Rows 6–21: Rep rows 2–5 consecutively. *(16 [18, 20, 22] dc)*
Rows 22–26: Rep row 2.

Armhole & Neck Shaping
Row 27: Sl st in each of first 4 [4, 5, 5] sts, ch 3, dc in each st across to last 2 sts, dc dec in next 2 sts, turn. *(12 [14, 15, 17] dc)*
Row 28: Ch 2, dc in each rem st across, turn. *(11 [13, 14, 16] dc)*
Row 29: Ch 3, dc in each st across to last 2 sts, dc dec in next 2 sts, turn. *(10 [12, 13, 15] dc)*
Rows 30 & 31 [30–32, 30–32, 30–33]: Rep rows 28 and 29 alternately. *(8 [9, 10, 11] dc)*
Rows 32 & 33 [33, 33–35, 34 & 35]: Rep row 2. At the end of last rep, fasten off.

Right Front
Rows 1–4: Rep rows 1–4 of Left Front. *(21 [23, 25, 27] dc)*
Row 5: Ch 3, dc in each dc across to last 2 dc, dc dec in next 2 sts, turn. *(20 [22, 24, 26] dc)*
Row 6: Ch 3, dc in each st across, turn.
Rows 7 & 8: Rep row 6.
Rows 9–24: Rep rows 5–8 consecutively. *(16 [18, 20, 22] dc)*
Rows 25 & 26: Rep row 6.

CONTINUED ON PAGE 144

HEARTFELT BAG

Wear your heart on your shoulder in eye-catching style with this trendy, cute-as-can-be felted purse that gets an extra dose of dimension with luxurious eyelash yarn.

INTERMEDIATE

Finished Size

After felting: 7 x 9 inches, excluding Strap

4 MEDIUM

5 BULKY

Materials

- Lion Brand Lion Wool medium (worsted) weight yarn (3 oz/185 yds/85g per skein):
    1 skein #140 rose
- Lion brand Fun Fur bulky (chunky) weight eyelash yarn (1¾ oz/ 60 yds/50g per skein):
    2 skeins #195 hot pink
- Size P/16/11.5mm crochet hook or size needed to obtain gauge
- Large-eyed blunt tapestry needle
- Sewing needle
- Sewing thread
- Lingerie bag
- Washer
- Dryer
- Laundry detergent

Gauge

Before felting: 12 sts = 5 inches; 9 rows = 4 inches

CONTINUED ON PAGE 144

NORTHERN LIGHTS
SCARF & MITTENS

A sophisticated mix of wool and mohair yarns accented with metallic highlights gives glamorous style with a bit of bling to this ultra-chic winter set.

INTERMEDIATE

5 BULKY

Finished Sizes

Mittens: Adult
Scarf: 6 x 53 inches
    excluding Fringe

Materials

- Various black wool, mohair and chenille bulky (chunky) weight yarns:
    - 3 oz/105 yds/84g black wool
    - 2 oz/70 yds/56g each chenille, mohair with metallic thread and eyelash
- Size P/16/11.5mm crochet hook or size needed to obtain gauge
- Yarn needle
- 2 stitch markers

Gauge

6 dc = 3 inches; 2 sc rnds = 1 inch

Pattern Notes

Weave in loose ends as work progresses.
Join rounds with a slip stitch unless otherwise stated.

CONTINUED ON PAGE 147

WINTER BLUES

Cotton terry chenille yarn gives soft, cozy comfort to this stylish set that's easy enough for a beginner. Chic ribbon rosettes add the perfect finishing touch!

EASY

5 BULKY

Finished Sizes

Bust: 32 inches (small)
Length: 27 inches from back neck to bottom edge.
Hat: Adult

Gauge

With Size P hook and chenille: 5 sc = 3 inches; 4 rows = 2 inches

Pattern Notes

Weave in loose ends as work progresses.
Join rounds with a slip stitch unless otherwise stated.

Materials

- Crystal Palace Cotton Chenille Yarns bulky (chunky) weight yarn:
   12 oz/420 yds/340g blue
- 4 oz/140 yds/113g novelty white bulky yarn
- Sizes K/10½/6.5mm and P/16/11.5mm crochet hooks or size needed to obtain gauge
- Yarn needle
- Sewing needle
- White sewing thread
- ¼-inch-wide white ribbon: 7 yds
- 15mm white shank button

VEST

Lower Body

Row 1: With size P hook and blue, ch 69, sc in 2nd ch from hook, sc in each rem ch across, turn. *(68 sc)*

Row 2: Ch 1, sc in each sc across, turn.

Rows 3–32: Rep row 2.

Right Front

Row 1: Ch 1, sc in each of next 15 sc, turn. *(15 sc)*

Row 2: Ch 1, sc in next 14 sc, turn.

Row 3: Ch 1, sc in each of next 13 sc, turn.

Row 4: Ch 1, sc in each of next 12 sc, turn.

Row 5: Ch 1, sc in each of next 10 sc, turn.

Rows 6–20: Ch 1, sc in each of next 9 sc, turn. At the end of row 20, fasten off.

Left Front

Row 1: Attach blue in first sc of row 32 of Lower Body, ch 1, sc in each of next 15 sc, turn. *(15 sc)*

Rows 2–20: Rep rows 2–20 of Right Front.

Back

Row 1: Working in rem sts of row 32 of Lower Body, sk next 9 sc, attach blue in next sc, ch 1, sc in same sc as beg ch-1, sc in each of next 19 sc, turn, leaving rem 9 sc unworked. *(20 sc)*

Rows 2–20: Ch 1, sc in each of next 20 sc, turn At the end of last rep, fasten off.

Trim

Rnd 1: With size P hook, attach white novelty yarn at center back neck, ch 1, sc evenly sp around entire outer edge of vest, join in beg sc, fasten off.

Rosette

Rnd 1: With size K hook and white ribbon, ch 4, sl st in first ch to form a ring, ch 1, 12 sc in ring, join in beg sc. *(12 sc)*

Rnd 2: Ch 3 *(counts as first dc)* dc in same sc as beg ch-3, ch 1, sk 1 sc, [2 dc in next sc, ch 1, sk 1 sc] around, join in 3rd ch of beg ch-3. *(6 ch-1 sps)*

Rnd 3: Sl st into ch-1 sp, ch 1, sc in same ch-1 sp, ch 5, [sc in next ch-1 sp, ch 5] around, join in beg sc. *(6 ch-5 sps)*

Rnd 4: Ch 1, work (sc, hdc, dc, hdc, sc) in each ch-5 sp around, join in beg sc, fasten off. *(6 petals)*

Finishing

Cut a 6-inch length of white ribbon, fold ribbon in half and knot ends tog, sew center of fold to back of Rosette. With sewing needle and thread, sew Rosette to edge of row 4 of Right Front. Sew button on inside edge opposite the Rosette.

HAT

Rnd 1 (WS): With size P hook and blue, ch 4, sl st to join in first ch to form a ring, ch 3 *(counts as first dc)*, 11 dc in ring, join in 3rd ch of beg ch-3, turn. *(12 dc)*

Rnd 2: Ch 3, dc in same st as beg ch-3, 2 dc in each rem st around, join in 3rd ch of beg ch-3, turn. *(24 dc)*

Rnd 3: Rep rnd 2. *(48 dc)*

Rnd 4: Ch 3, dc in each of next 3 dc, **fpdc** *(see Stitch Guide)* around each of next 4 dc, [dc in each of next 4 dc, fpdc around each of next 4 dc] around, join in 3rd

CONTINUED ON PAGE 146

LEAPIN' LIZARDS!

Worked in eye-popping, gecko green in a textured pattern of popcorn and cluster stitches, this fanciful scarf makes a fun accessory for your winter wardrobe.

INTERMEDIATE

5 BULKY

Finished Size

5 x 63 inches

Materials

- Yarn Bee Icelandic Jewels bulky (chunky) weight yarn (3½ oz/129 yds/100g per skein):
    2 skeins #26 peridot
- Size P/16/11.5mm crochet hook or size needed to obtain gauge
- Yarn needle

Gauge

3 sc = 1½ inches

Pattern Notes

Weave in loose ends as work progresses.
Join rounds with a slip stitch unless otherwise stated.

Special Stitches

4-double crochet cluster (4-dc cl): (Yo, insert hook in indicated sp, yo, draw up a lp, yo, draw through 2 lps on hook) 4 times in same sp, yo, draw through all 5 lps on hook.

Popcorn (pc): 4 dc in indicated st, draw up a lp, remove hook, insert hook in first dc of 4-dc group,

CONTINUED ON PAGE 146

PIZZAZZ ON THE PRAIRIE

There's nothing "plain" about this jazzy purse stitched in luscious bulky weight yarn and accented with fashion yarns to kick it up a notch in dazzling style.

INTERMEDIATE

BULKY 5

Finished Sizes

Purse: 7½ x 8 inches,
    excluding Shoulder Strap
Front Motif: 6 inches

Gauge

4 sc = 2½ inches

Materials

- Lion Brand Homespun bulky (chunky) weight yarn (6 oz/185 yds/170g per skein):
    1 skein #335 prairie
- Bulky (chunky) weight yarn:
    2 oz/54 yds/58g magenta/metallic gold
- Size P/16/11.5mm crochet hook or size needed to obtain gauge
- Yarn needle

Pattern Notes

Weave in loose ends as work progresses.
Join rounds with a slip stitch unless otherwise stated.

Special Stitches

3-double crochet cluster (3-dc cl): (Yo, insert hook in indicated sp, yo, draw up a lp, yo, draw through 2 lps on hook) 3 times in same sp, yo, draw through all 4 lps on hook, ch 1 to lock.

Beginning 3-double crochet cluster (beg 3-dc cl): Ch 2, (yo, insert hook in same st as beg ch-2, yo, draw up a lp, yo, draw through 2 lps on hook) twice, yo, draw through all 3 lps on hook.

Puff stitch (puff st): (Yo, insert hook in st, yo, draw up a lp) 3 times in same st or sp *(7 lps on hook)*, yo, draw through all lp on hook, ch 1 to lock.

Purse Front Flap

Rnd 1 (RS): With magenta/gold, ch 5, join with sl

CONTINUED ON PAGE 147

FRUIT FANTASY HAT

Simple crochet stitches mix it up with thick, thin and furry yarns to cast a magical spell of design and texture in this delectably soft hat worked in yummy fruit colors.

EASY

Finished Size
One size fits most:
  8 inches long
  x 17 inches in diameter
  unstretched

6
SUPER BULKY

2
FINE

Materials
- Tahki Yarns Ghost Print super bulky (super chunky) weight yarn (65 yds/100g per skein):
  1 skein #4103 rose
- Brazilia Fantasy by Schachenmayr Yarn fine (sport) weight yarn (1¾ oz/99 yds/50g):
  1 skein #383 peach/ orange/gold/rose
- Size P/16/11.5mm crochet hook or size needed to obtain gauge
- Yarn needle
- Stitch marker

Gauge
(Sc, ch 2, sc) 4 times = 4 inches

Pattern Notes
Weave in loose ends as work progresses.
Do not join rounds unless otherwise stated.
Use a stitch marker to mark rounds.

Hat
Rnd 1 (RS): With rose, ch 2, (sc, ch 2, sc) 4 times in 2nd ch from hook, place st marker. *(8 sc; 4 ch-2 sps)*

Rnd 2: [(Sc, ch 2, sc) twice in next ch-2 sp] 4 times. *(16 sc; 8 ch-2 sps)*

Rnd 3: [(Sc, ch 2, sc) in next ch-2 sp, (sc, ch 2, sc) twice in next ch-2 sp] 4 times. *(24 sc; 12 ch-2 sps)*

Rnd 4: (Sc, ch 2, sc) in each ch-2 sp around.

Rnds 5–8: Rep rnd 4.

Rnd 9: Continuing with rose, add a strand of fantasy Mexico, to join both strands tog, sl st in next ch-2 sp, ch 1, (sc, ch 2, sc) in same ch-2 sp, (sc, ch 2, sc) in each rem ch-2 sp around.

Rnds 10–12: Rep rnd 4. At the end of rnd 12, fasten off. ❖

BOUDOIR ELEGANCE PILLOW

Stitched in beautiful textured yarn with a hint of sparkle, this dazzling pillow created in Tunisian knit stitch is sure to add some colorful spice to a lady's bedroom.

INTERMEDIATE

Finished Size

14 inches square

5 BULKY

Materials

- Moda Dea Caché bulky (chunky) weight yarn (1¾ oz/72 yds/50g per skein): 5 skeins #2355 siren
- Size P/16/11.5mm Easy Tunisian™ crochet hook or size needed to obtain gauge
- Yarn needle
- 14-inch pillow form
- Fancy broach

Gauge

8 sts = 4 inches

Pattern Notes

Weave in loose ends as work progresses.
Join rounds with a slip stitch unless otherwise stated.

Special Stitches

Tunisian knit stitch (tks): Sk first vertical bar, [insert hook through center of the st to back of piece, yo, draw up a lp] across retaining all lps on hook.
Return: Yo, draw through first lp on hook, [yo,

CONTINUED ON PAGE 147

MISTY MEADOWS

The soft, soothing colors of a country garden come alive in this beautiful floral throw stitched in deliciously soft super-bulky yarn that begs to be snuggled!

INTERMEDIATE

SUPER BULKY

Finished Size
44 x 63 inches

Materials
- Red Heart Light & Lofty super bulky (super chunky) weight yarn (6 oz/140 yds/170g per skein):
    - 4 skeins #9334 café au lait
    - 3 skeins #9631 sage
    - 2 skeins #9632 pine
    - 1 skein each #9372 antique rose, #9531 plum and #9380 antique blue
- Red Heart Baby Clouds super bulky (super chunky) weight yarn (4½ oz/105 yds/127g per skein):
    - 1 skein #9341 yellow swirl
- Size P/16/11.5mm afghan crochet hook or size needed to obtain gauge
- Size N/15/10mm crochet hook
- Yarn needle

Gauge
Size P hook: 6 sts = 3 inches; 6 rows = 3 inches

Pattern Notes
Weave in loose ends as work progresses.
Join rounds with a slip stitch unless otherwise stated.

Special Stitches
3-double crochet cluster (3-dc cl): [Yo, insert hook in indicated sp, yo, draw up a lp, yo, draw through 2 lps on hook] 3 times in same sp, yo, draw through all 4 lps on hook, ch 1 to lock.

Tunisian knit stitch (tks): [With yarn in back, insert hook front to back between both vertical strands of next st, yo, draw yarn through st] across retaining all lps on hook.

Return: Yo, draw yarn through 1 lp on hook, [yo, draw through 2 lps on hook] across until 1 lp rem on hook.

Panel
Make 1 each of the 3 charts.

Row 1: With size P afghan hook and café au lait, ch 21, working from right to left, insert hook in 2nd ch from hook, yo, draw up a lp, [insert hook in next ch, yo, draw up a lp] across retaining all lps on hook

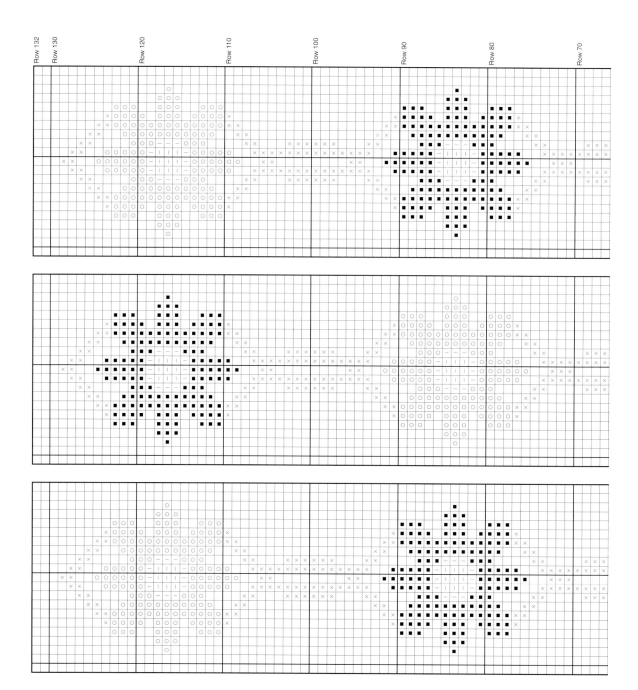

(21 lps on hook), yo, draw through 1 lp on hook, [yo, draw through 2 lps on hook] across until 1 lp rem on hook and this counts as first lp of next row throughout.

Rows 2 & 3: Work **tks** *(see Special Stitches)* *(21 lps on hook)*, **return** *(see Special Stitches)*.

Rows 4–132: Working in Tunisian knit st, follow chart, changing color as chart indicates, when working return, **change color** *(see Stitch Guide)* matching sts being removed.

Row 133: Working through both lps of each vertical st, sl st in each st across, fasten off.

Side Border

Row 1: Working down length, with size N hook, attach café au lait in first row-end st, ch 1, sc in first 5 row end sts, *sk next row, sc in each of next 5 row end sts, rep from * across to last row, sc in last row, fasten off.

Row 2: Attach sage in first sc of previous row, ch 3 *(counts as first dc)*, dc in each sc across, fasten off.

Row 3: Attach café au lait in top of beg ch-3 of previous row, ch 3, **fpdc** *(see Stitch Guide)* around the vertical post of each dc across, fasten off.

Rep rows 1–4 on opposite long edge of Panel.

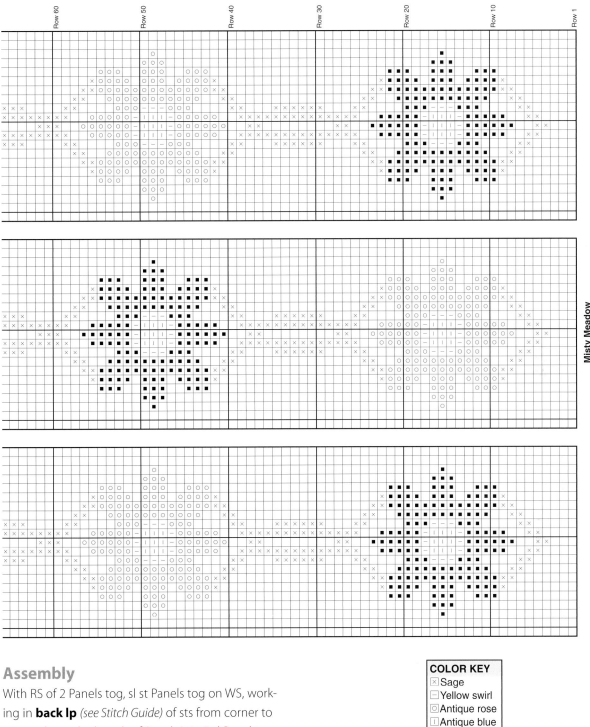

Row 60　Row 50　Row 40　Row 30　Row 20　Row 10　Row 1

Misty Meadow

Assembly

With RS of 2 Panels tog, sl st Panels tog on WS, work-ing in **back lp** (see Stitch Guide) of sts from corner to corner down the length of Panel. Join 3rd Panel to joined panels.

Top & Bottom Border

Row 1: With RS facing, with size N hook, attach pine in top right-hand corner, ch 3, dc in corner row end st, 2 dc in next row end st, *dc in each of next 2 rows, dc in each of next 2 sts, [sk next st, dc in each of next 3 sts] 4 times, sk next st, dc in each of next 2 sts, dc in

each of next 2 row end sts, 2 dc in next row end st**, dc in each of next 2 row end sts, 2 dc in next row end st, rep from * across, ending last rep at **, 2 dc in last row end st, fasten off.
Rep row 1 across bottom of Throw. ❖

COLOR KEY
⊠ Sage
☐ Yellow swirl
◉ Antique rose
❘ Antique blue
■ Plum

CALIENTE

A spicy blend of hot salsa colors gives zesty style to this vibrant throw that will add a festive splash to any contemporary setting from a loft to a penthouse.

INTERMEDIATE

Finished Size
55 x 61 inches

Gauge
8 sts = 4 inches; 8 rows = 4 inches

Materials
- Red Heart Light & Lofty super bulky (super chunky) weight yarn (4½ oz/105 yds/127g per skein):
  7 skeins #9914 glow (A)
- Red Heart Super Saver medium (worsted) weight yarn (5 oz/278 yds/141g per skein):
  2 skeins #413 farmland (B)
- TLC Amoré medium (worsted) weight yarn (6 oz/278 yds/170g per skein):
  1 skein each #3628 dark thyme (C) and #3254 persimmon (D)
- Size P/16/11.5mm crochet hook or size needed to obtain gauge
- Large-eyed blunt needle

Pattern Notes
Weave in loose ends as work progresses.
Join rounds with a slip stitch unless otherwise stated.

Throw
Row 1: With A, ch 100, dc in 5th ch from hook, dc in each of next 4 chs, [3 dc in next ch, dc in each of next 5 chs, yo, draw up a lp in next ch, yo, draw through 2 lps on hook, sk next ch, yo, draw up a lp in next ch, yo, draw through 2 lps on hook (3 lps on hook), yo, draw through all 3 lps on hook, sc in next 5 chs] across, ending with dc in last ch, turn.

Row 2: Ch 3 (counts as first dc), sk next dc, *dc in each of next 5 dc, 3 dc in next dc, dc in each of next 5 dc**, yo, draw up a lp in next dc, yo, draw through 2 lps on hook, sk 1 dc, yo, draw up a lp in next dc, yo, draw through 2 lps on hook, yo, draw through all 3 lps on hook, dc in each of next 5 dc, rep from * across, ending last rep at **, sk 1 dc, dc in last dc, fasten off.

Row 3: With 2 strands of B, rep row 2.

Row 4: Rep row 2, fasten off.

Row 5: With A, rep row 2.

Row 6: Rep row 2, fasten off.

Row 7: With 1 strand each C and D, rep row 2.

Row 8: Rep row 2, fasten off.

Row 9: With A, rep row 2.

Row 10: Rep row 2, fasten off.
Rows 11–50: Rep rows 3–10.

Edging
Row 1 (RS): With 1 strand each C and D held tog,

attach in side edge of yarn, ch 1, sc evenly sp across long side edge of Throw, fasten off.
Rep row 1 on opposite long edge of Throw. ❖

CASCADES

A soft, subtle ripple design highlighted in cream against a background of deep blue creates the impression of a gently cascading waterfall in this cozy throw.

EASY

SUPER BULKY

Finished Size
46 x 62 inches

Materials
- Red Heart Light & Lofty super bulky (super chunky) weight yarn (6 oz/140 yds/170g per skein):
    6 skeins #9380 antique blue
    1 skein #9334 café au lait
- Size P/16/11.5mm crochet hook or size needed to obtain gauge
- Yarn needle

Gauge
4 dc = 2¾ inches

Pattern Notes
Weave in loose ends as work progresses.
Join rounds with a slip stitch unless otherwise stated.

Throw
Row 1 (RS): With antique blue, ch 85, dc in 4th ch from hook, dc in each of next 3 chs, sk next 2 chs, dc in each of next 3 chs, [(dc, ch 2, dc) in next ch, dc in each of next 3 chs, sk next 2 chs, dc in each of next 3 chs] 8 times, 2 dc in last ch, turn.

Row 2 (WS): Ch 3 (counts as first dc), working in **front lps** (see Stitch Guide) only, dc in same st as beg ch-3, dc in each of next 3 sts, sk next 2 sts, dc in each of next 3 sts, [dc in first ch of ch-2 sp, ch 2, dc in 2nd ch of ch-2 sp, dc in each of next 3 sts, sk next 2 sts, dc in each of next 3 sts] 8 times, 2 dc in last st, draw up a lp, remove hook and drop yarn, do not fasten off.

Row 3 (RS): Working in rem free **back lps** (see Stitch Guide) of each st, attach café au lait with sl st in first st, ch 1, sc in same st, sc in each st and each ch across, fasten off, do not turn.

Note: *When working row 4, sk sc sts of previous row unless otherwise indicated to work in specific sts.*

Row 4 (RS): Pick up dropped lp of antique blue, ch 3, dc in first sc of previous row, dc in each of next 3 dc, [dc in sc worked in first ch, ch 2, dc in sc worked in 2nd ch, dc in each of next 3 dc, sk next 2 dc, dc in each of next 3 dc] across, ending with dc in last sc of previous row, dc in last dc, turn.

Rows 5 & 6: Ch 3, dc in same st as beg ch-3, dc in each of next 3 dc, sk each of next 2 dc, dc in each of next 3 dc, [(dc, ch 2, dc) in next ch-2 sp, dc in each of next 3 dc, sk each of next 2 dc, dc in each of next 3 dc] across, 2 dc in last dc, turn.

Rows 7–46: Rep rows 2–6 consecutively.

Rows 47–49: Rep rows 2–4. At the end of row 49, fasten off. ❧

MAY BASKET

Celebrate the old-world tradition of pretty May Baskets with this beautiful design crocheted with strips of fabric in a fresh, springtime floral pattern.

INTERMEDIATE

Finished Size
4½ inches tall x 8½ inches deep x 14 inches wide, excluding Handles

Gauge
Rnds 1–3 = 6 inches; 3 sc = 2 inches

Pattern Notes
Weave in loose ends as work progresses.

Join rounds with a slip stitch unless otherwise stated.

Materials
- The Quiltmakers Garden fabric, designed by Suzan Ellis for Northcott (44-inches-wide):
    3½ yds #665 Katie Herling Tulips
- Size P/16/11.5mm crochet hook or size needed to obtain gauge
- Sewing needle
- Sewing thread
- Stitch markers

Fabric Preparation
Cutting along the straight edge, cut fabric into 20 strips 2 inches wide x 42 inches long, rem piece of fabric will be 4 x 42 inches long.

Cut an up-and-down slit ½ inch long in both ends of every strip starting ½ inch from end and 1 inch in from each side and ending 1 inch from end and 1 inch in from each side.

To connect strips, with right sides facing up, place beg of 2nd strip over end of first strip, line slits up, going from bottom to top, push end of 2nd strip up through slit. Pull strips to tighten connection.

For less fraying of fabric, fold raw edges of strip toward center, then fold strip in half lengthwise to encase raw edges as crocheting progresses.

For more fraying of fabric, fold strip in half lengthwise twice as crocheting progresses.

Basket
Rnd 1 (RS): Ch 6, join with sl st in first ch to form

ring, ch 1, work 12 sc in ring, do not join, use st marker to mark rnds. *(12 sc)*

Rnd 2: Working in **back lp** *(see Stitch Guide)* only, work 2 sc in each st around. *(24 sc)*

Rnd 3: Working in back lps only, [2 sc in next st, sc in next st] 12 times, sl st in next st. *(36 sc)*

Rnd 4: Ch 1, working in **front lps** *(see Stitch Guide)* only, sc in each st around, join in beg sc, turn.

Rnd 5: Ch 1, sc in each sc around, do not join. *(36 sc)*

Rnd 6: Sc in each sc around.

Rnd 7: *[2 sc in next sc, sc in next sc] 4 times, sc in next sc, **sc dec** *(see Stitch Guide)* in next 2 sc, sc in each of next 3 sc, sc dec in next 2 sc, sc in each of next 2 sc, rep from *. *(40 sc)*

Rnd 8: Sc in next 3 sc, [2 sc in next sc, sc in next sc] 3 times, sc in next 14 sc, [2 sc in next sc, sc in next sc] 3 times, sc in next 11 sc. *(46 sc)*

Rnd 9: Sc in each of next 5 sc, *2 sc in each of next 4 sts, sc in each of next 8 sc *(place a st marker on last st)*, sc in each of next 4 sc *(place a st marker on last st)**,

sc in each of next 7 sc, rep bet *, sc in each of next 2 sc, sl st in next st, fasten off. *(54 sc)*

Handles

Attach fabric in first marked st on rnd 9, ch 30, sl st in last marked st of rnd 9, fasten off. Attach fabric in 2nd marked st on rnd 9, ch 30, sl st in 3rd marked st on rnd 9, fasten off.

Handle Clasp

Cut a strip of fabric 4 x 10-inches, fold in half so that piece measures 4 x 5 inches. To prevent fraying, fold cut edges in and sew in place. Wrap fabric around top of both handles on basket, then sew fabric ends tog encasing handles in between.

Bow

Cut 2 strips of fabric 1 x 26 inches, attach 1 strip to each side of basket between handles and tie each strip in a bow. ❖

BRANDYWINE CAPELET CONTINUED FROM PAGE 122

Capelet

Row 1: Holding 1 strand each chestnut and cognac tog, ch 93, sc in 2nd ch from hook,

sc in each rem ch across, turn. *(92 sc)*

Rows 2–26: Ch 1, sc in each sc across, turn. At the end of row 26, fasten off. ❖

DISCO DAZZLE CONTINUED FROM PAGE 123

side of foundation ch, [ch 20, sk next ch, sl st in next ch] 3 times, fasten off.

Headband

Rnd 1: With 1 strand of each color held tog, ch 30,

taking care not to twist, sl st in first ch to form a ring, ch 1, sc in same ch as beg ch-1, sc in each rem ch around, join in beg sc. *(30 sc)*

Rnd 2: Ch 1, sc in each sc around, join in beg sc, fasten off. ❖

BLUE LAGOON CONTINUED FROM PAGE 125

Armhole & Neck Shaping

Row 27: Ch 2, dc in next dc (beg dc dec), dc in each dc across to last 3 [3, 4, 4] sts, turn. *(12 [14, 15, 17] dc)*

Row 28: Rep row 5. *(11 [13, 14, 16] dc)*

Row 29: Ch 2, dc in next dc, dc in each rem dc across, turn. *(10 [12, 13, 15] dc)*

Rows 30 & 31 [30–32, 30–32, 30–33]: Rep rows 28 and 29 alternately. *(8 [9, 10, 11] dc)*

Rows 32 & 33 [33, 33–35, 34 & 35]: Rep row 6. At the end of last rep, fasten off.

Sleeve

Make 2.

Row 1: With 1 strand each lime blue and turquoise held tog, ch 28 [28, 33, 33] dc in 4th ch from hook, dc in each rem ch across, turn. *(26 [26, 31, 31] dc)*

Rows 2–13 [13, 14, 14]: Ch 3, dc in each dc across, turn. At the end of last rep, fasten off.

Assembly

With yarn needle and blue yarn, sew shoulder seams. Set in Sleeves, sew in place and sew Sleeve and side seams.

Shawl Collar

Row 1: With RS facing, attach 1 strand each lime blue and turquoise with sl st in first st on Back neck after right shoulder seam, ch 1, sc in same st and in each st across Back neck, sc in next row end on Left Front neck, turn. *(9 [10, 9, 10] sc)*

Row 2: Ch 1, sc in each st across and in first row end at top of Right Front shoulder, turn. *(10 [11, 10, 11] sc)*

Row 3: Ch 1, sc across and in next end of row on Left Front shoulder, turn.

Continue in sc, working 1 extra sc st on each coat Front until 32 [33, 32, 33] sc, then continue in sc working 2 extra sc in ends of rows on each jacket Front until there are 40 [41, 44, 45] sc total, fasten off. Sew toggle or button to Left Front and use natural sp between dc sts of Right Front for buttonhole. ❧

HEARTFELT BAG CONTINUED FROM PAGE 126

Pattern Notes

Weave in loose ends as work progresses.
Join rounds with a slip stitch unless otherwise stated.
Bag is sewn tog before felting; the strap, button and loop are crocheted, felted and sewn on after felting.

Bag Side

Make 2.

Row 1: With 1 strand each yarn held tog, ch 3, sc in 2nd ch from hook, sc in next ch, turn. *(2 sc)*

Row 2: Ch 1, 2 sc in first sc, 2 sc in next sc, turn. *(4 sc)*

Row 3: Ch 1, 2 sc in first sc, sc in each sc across to last sc, 2 sc in last sc, turn. *(6 sc)*

Rows 4–12: Rep row 3. *(24 sc)*

Rows 13 & 14: Ch 1, sc in each sc across, turn.

First Lobe

Row 15: Ch 1, sc in each of next 12 sc, turn. *(12 sc)*

Row 16: Ch 1, **sc dec** *(see Stitch Guide)* in next 2 sc, sc in each sc across to last 2 sc, sc dec in next 2 sc, turn. *(10 sc)*

Rows 17–19: Rep row 16. *(4 sc)*

Row 20: Ch 1, [sc dec in next 2 sc] twice, fasten off. *(2 sc)*

2nd Lobe

Row 15: Attach 1 strand of each yarn in next un-worked sc of row 14, ch 1, sc in same sc as beg ch-1, sc in each of next 11 sc, turn. *(12 sc)*

Rows 16–20: Rep rows 16–20 of First Lobe.

Trim

Row 1: Attach 1 strand of each yarn in right-hand side in opposite side of foundation ch, ch 1, sc in same ch as beg ch-1, working up side edge of heart, work 27 sc evenly sp to center top of heart, turn. *(28 sc)*

Row 2: Ch 1, sc in each sc of previous row, fasten off.

Row 3: Attach 1 strand each color in left-hand side in opposite side of foundation ch, ch 1, sc in same ch as beg ch-1, work 27 sc up opposite side of heart, turn. *(28 sc)*

Row 4: Ch 1, sc in each sc of previous row, fasten off. With a length of rose and tapestry needle, sew heart sections tog, sewing from center bottom upward halfway across top of lobe. Rep sewing on opposite side of heart in same manner.

Strap

With 1 strand of each yarn held tog, ch 80, sl st in 2nd ch from hook, sl st in each rem ch across, fasten off.

Button

With 1 strand of each yarn held tog, leaving a length of each yarn at beg, ch 3, [yo, insert hook in first ch of ch-3, draw up a lp, yo, draw through 2 lps on hook]

3 times, yo, draw through all 4 lps on hook, leaving a length of yarn, fasten off. To form a rounded knot, tie beg and end tail tog, weave ends into inside of ball.

Loop

With 1 strand of each yarn held tog, ch 12, fasten off.

Felting

Turn Bag inside out, place Strap, Button and Loop inside the lingerie bag. Place bag in washing machine and wash in hot water with detergent for 2 cycles of 12 minutes each. Dry pieces thoroughly in dryer.

Finishing

With sewing needle and thread, sew Strap to each side of Bag at top of each side of Lobe. Sew Button at center front between Lobes, draw ends of lp into fabric on center back between Lobes and secure to fit over Button. ❖

NORTHERN LIGHTS SCARF & MITTENS CONTINUED FROM PAGE 127

MITTEN

Make 2.

Cuff

Rnd 1: Beg at cuff with mohair with metallic thread, ch 17 sl st in first ch to form a ring, ch 1, sc in each ch around, join in beg sc, turn. *(17 sc)*

Rnd 2: Ch 1, sc in each sc around, join in beg sc, turn.

Rnds 3–6: Rep rnd 2. At the end of rnd 6, fasten off.

Rnd 7: Attach black wool, ch 1, sc in each sc around, inc 2 sc evenly sp around, join in beg sc. *(19 sc)*

Rnds 8 & 9: Ch 1, sc in each sc around, join in beg sc.

Thumb

Rnd 10: Ch 1, sc in each of next 4 sc, ch 1, sk next 12 sc, sc in each of next 3 sc, join in beg sc, turn. *(7 sc; ch-1 sp)*

Rnd 11: Ch 1, sc in each of next 3 sc, sc in next ch-1, sc in each of next 4 sc, join, turn.

Rnd 12: Ch 1, sc in each sc around, join in beg sc, turn. Rep rnd 12 until thumb measures 2½ inches, leaving

a length of yarn, fasten off.

Hand

Rnd 10: Attach black wool in next unworked sc of rnd 9, ch 1, work 18 sc around palm, working in rem sc of rnd 9, in side edge of thumb sts and in ch-1 sp of thumb, join in beg sc, turn. *(18 sc)*

Rnds 11–14: Ch 1, sc in each sc around, join in beg sc, turn.

Rnd 15: Place mitten flat, place a st marker at each side edge of mitten, ch 1, [sc in each sc to within 1 st of marker, **sc dec** *(see Stitch Guide)* in next 2 sc] twice, sc in each rem sc, join, turn. *(16 sc)*

Rnds 16–22: Ch 1, sc in each sc around, join in beg sc, turn.

Rnd 23: Ch 1, sc in each sc around, working sc dec at each side edge of palm, join in beg sc, turn. *(14 sc)*

Rnd 24: Ch 1, sc in each sc around, join in beg sc, turn.

Rnd 25: Ch 1, sc dec in next 2 sc, [sc in next sc, sc dec in next 2 sc] around, join in beg sc, leaving a length of

yarn, fasten off.
Turn Mitten WS out, weave through sts of rnd 25, pull to close opening, fasten off. Weave length through sts of Thumb, pull to close opening, secure, fasten off. Turn Mitten RS out.

SCARF

Row 1: With black wool, ch 102, dc in 4th ch from hook, dc in each rem ch across, fasten off, turn. *(100 dc)*

Rows 2–7: Attach another texture of black yarn, ch 3 *(counts as first dc)*, dc in each dc across, fasten off, turn.

Fringe

Cut lengths of yarn in 12 inch lengths, fold 2 strands in half, insert hook in end of row, draw strands through at fold to form a lp on hook, draw cut ends through lp on hook, pull gently to secure. Attach Fringe in each row on each end of scarf. ❖

WINTER BLUES CONTINUED FROM PAGE 129

ch of beg ch-3, turn. *(24 dc; 24 fpdc)*

Rnd 5: Ch 3, **bpdc** *(see Stitch Guide)* around each post st and dc in each dc around, join in 3rd ch of beg ch-3, turn.

Rnd 6: Ch 3, dc in each dc around and fpdc around each post st, join in 3rd ch of beg ch-3, turn.

Rnds 7–10: Rep rnds 5 and 6 alternately. At the end of rnd 10, fasten off blue yarn.

Rnd 11 (RS): With size P hook, draw up a lp of white novelty yarn, ch 1, sc in each st around, join in beg sc. *(48 sc)*

Rnd 12: Ch 1, sc in each sc around, join in beg sc, fasten off.

Rosette

Rnds 1–4: Rep rnds 1–4 of Vest Rosette.

Small Rosette

Rnd 1: With size K hook and white ribbon, ch 4, sl st to join in first ch to form a ring, ch 1, work 12 sc sts in ring, join in beg sc. *(12 sc)*

Rnd 2: Ch 5 *(counts as first dc, ch 2)*, sk next sc, [dc in next sc, ch 2, sk next sc] around, join in 3rd ch of beg ch-5. *(6 ch-2 sps)*

Rnd 3: Ch 1, (sc, hdc, dc, hdc, sc) in each ch-2 sp around, join in beg sc, fasten off. *(6 petals)*

With sewing needle and thread, sew Rosette to rnd 7 and Small Rosette next to and slightly below onto rnd 8. ❖

LEAPIN' LIZARDS CONTINUED FROM PAGE 130

pick up dropped lp and draw through st on hook.

Scarf

Row 1: Ch 102, sc in 2nd ch from hook, sc in each rem ch across, turn. *(101 sc)*

Row 2: Ch 1, sc in same sc as beg ch-1, sc in next sc, [**4-dc cl** *(see Special Stitches)* in next sc, sc in each of next 3 sc] 24 times, 4-dc cl in next sc, sc in each of next 2 sc, fasten off, do not turn. *(25 dc cls; 76 sc)*

Row 3: Attach yarn in first sc of previous row, ch 1, sc in same sc as beg ch-1, sc in next sc, sc in top of 4-dc cl, sc in next sc *(4 sc completed)*, [4-dc cl in next sc, sc in each of next 3 sts] across, ending with sc in each of last 4 sts, fasten off, do not turn. *(24 dc cl; 77 sc)*

Row 4: Attach yarn in first sc of previous row, ch 1, sc in same sc as beg ch-1, sc in next sc, [4-dc cl in next sc, sc in each of next 3 sts] 24 times, 4-dc cl in next st, sc in each of next 2 sts, fasten off, do not turn. *(25 dc cl; 76 sc)*

Rows 5 & 6: Rep rows 3 and 4.

Row 7: With RS facing, attach yarn in right corner, working in ends of rows, ch 1, work 5 sc evenly sp across ends of rows, fasten off. (5 sc)

Rep row 7 on opposite end of scarf.

Rnd 8: Now working in rnds, with RS facing, attach yarn in bottom right corner of scarf, *ch 3, **pc** (see Special Stitches) in same st as beg ch-3, ch 1, sl st in each of next 2 sts, rep from * around outer edge of scarf, working 3 pc on each end of scarf and 50 pc on each long edge of scarf, join at base of beg ch-3, fasten off. (106 pc) ♣

PIZZAZZ ON THE PRAIRIE CONTINUED FROM PAGE 131

st in first ch to form a ring, **beg 3-dc cl** (see Special Stitches) in ring, ch 3, [**3-dc cl** (see Special Stitches) in ring, ch 3] 5 times, join in top of beg 3-dc cl. (6 ch-3 sps; 6 cls)

Rnd 2: Sl st into ch-3 sp, (beg 3-dc cl, ch 2, 3-dc cl) in same ch-3 sp, ch 2, [(3-dc cl, ch 2, 3-dc cl) in next ch-3 sp, ch 2] around, join in top of beg 3-dc cl, fasten off. (12 ch-2 sps; 12 cls)

Rnd 3: Attach prairie in ch-2 sp between 2 groups of dc cls, ch 1, [3 sc in ch-2 sp between groups of dc cls, (3 sc, ch 2, 3 sc) in next ch-2 sp] around, join in beg sc, leaving a length of yarn, fasten off.

Purse Body

Row 1: With prairie, ch 13, sc in 2nd ch from hook, sc in each rem ch across, turn. (12 sc)

Row 2: Ch 1, hdc in each sc across, turn. (12 hdc)

Row 3: Ch 1, hdc in each hdc across, turn.

Rows 4–23: Rep row 3.

Row 24: Ch 1, sc in each hdc across, leaving a length of yarn, fasten off.

Fold row 1 to row 24, do not sew row 1 and row 24, sew only side seams. Sew Purse Front Flap to row 24.

Shoulder Strap

Row 1: With magenta/gold, ch 61, sc in 2nd ch from hook, sc in each rem ch across, fasten off. (60 sc)

Rnd 2: Now working in rnds, attach prairie in first sc of previous row, ch 1, sc in same sc as beg ch-1, sc in each of next 59 sc, 2 sc in end of row 1, working on opposite side of foundation ch of row 1, sc in each of next 60 chs, 2 sc in end of row 1, join in beg sc, fasten off. (124 sc)

Sew each end of Shoulder Strap to inside edge of Purse Body. ♣

BOUDOIR ELEGANCE PILLOW CONTINUED FROM PAGE 133

draw through 2 lps on hook] across until 1 lp remains on hook.

Pillow

Make 2.

Foundation: Ch 31, sc in 2nd ch from hook, sc in each rem ch across, turn. (30 sc)

Row 1: Work **tks** (see Special Stitches) across (31 lps on hook), work **return** (see Special Stitches) across sts.

Rows 2–29: Rep row 1.

Row 30: Sk first vertical bar, [insert hook from back to front between strands of next vertical bar, yo, draw up a lp, yo, draw through 2 lps on hook] across, fasten off.

Note: When 2nd Pillow piece is completed, do not fasten off.

Border

Rnd 1: Holding WS of Pillow sections tog, ch 1, [3 sc in corner st, sc evenly sp across to next corner] 3 times, insert pillow form, work 3 sc in next corner, sc in each sc across 4th edge, join in beg sc.

Rnd 2: Ch 1, work 2 sc in each sc around, join in beg sc, fasten off. ♣

SIMPLY SPECTAC-Q-LAR

From soft and muted to bold and bright,
you'll love how quickly these designs work up!
Featuring luxurious yarns in varying weights,
there's a little something for everyone.

WATERCOLOR STRIPES PULLOVER

The lightweight cotton yarn used in this striped pullover will keep you cool even when the temperature's hot.

EASY

MEDIUM 4

Finished Sizes
Small [medium, large]

Finished Garment Measurements
Bust: 38 [40, 42] inches

Gauge
Size Q hook: 5 sts = 4 inches; 6 rows = 3 inches

Pattern Notes
Weave in loose ends as work progresses.
Join rounds with a slip stitch unless otherwise stated.
Pullover is crocheted vertically.

Back
Row 1: Holding 1 strand each color tog, ch 26 [27,

Materials
- Tahki Cotton Classic II medium (worsted) weight yarn (1¾ oz/74 yds/50g per skein):
    4 [4, 5] skeins each
        #2815 turquoise,
        #2882 periwinkle and
        #2726 green
- Sizes L/11/8mm and Q/16mm crochet hooks or size needed to obtain gauge
- Tapestry needle
- ¾-inch turquoise shank button
- Stitch marker

28], sc in 2nd ch from hook, sc in each rem ch across, turn. *(25 [26, 27] sc)*

Row 2: Ch 1 *(counts as first sc)*, sk first st, working in **back lp** *(see Stitch Guide)* of each st, sc in each st across, ending with sc in top of end ch, place a st marker in last st to mark as top edge of Pullover, turn. *(25 [26, 27] sc)*

Rep row 2 until back measures 19 [20, 21] inches from beg, ending with last rep at bottom edge of Back *(opposite edge of st marker)*, fasten off.

Front
Row 1: Rep row 1 of Back.
Row 2: Rep row 2 of Back.
Rep row 2 until Front measures 9½ [10, 10½] inches from beg, ending at top edge of Front.

Neck Shaping
Row 1: Sl st in each of next 9 [10, 10] sts, sc in back lp of each of rem 16 [16, 17] sts, turn.
Row 2: Ch 1, sc in back lp of each of next 16 [16, 17] sts, ch 10 [11, 11], turn.
Row 3: Sk first ch, sc in each ch across, sc in back lp of each of next 16 [16, 17] sts, turn. *(25 [26, 27] sc)*
Rep row 2 of Back until Front measures 19 [20, 21] inches from beg, ending with last rep at bottom edge of Front, fasten off.

CONTINUED ON PAGE 170

SHADES OF TWILIGHT JACKET

Wrap yourself in cozy luxury with a fashionable jacket created in warm jewel-tones.

Finished Sizes
Small [medium, large]
Bust: 32–34 [36–38, 40–42] inches

Finished Garment Measurements
Bust: 38 [42, 48] inches

Gauge
6 sts = 5 inches; 9 rows = 7 inches

Pattern Notes
Weave in loose ends as work progresses.
Entire Jacket is crocheted holding 1 strand each color together.

Back
Row 1: Holding 1 strand each color tog, ch 24 [26, 30], sc in 2nd ch from hook, sc in each rem ch across, turn. *(23 [25, 29] sc)*

Materials
• Patons Allure bulky (chunky) weight yarn (1¾ oz/47 yds per ball): 9 [10, 12] balls each #04310 amethyst, #04405 ruby and #04208 turquoise
• Size Q/16mm crochet hook or size needed to obtain gauge
• Tapestry needle
• Smooth medium (worsted) weight yarn for seaming: 10 yds

Row 2: Ch 1, sc in each sc across, turn.
Rows 3–18: Rep row 2.

Armhole Shaping
Row 19: Sl st in each of first 3 [3, 4] sc, ch 1, sc in same st as last sl st, sc in each sc across to last 2 [2, 3] sc, turn, leaving rem sts unworked. *(19 [21, 23] sc)*
Rows 20–28 [20–28, 20–30]: Rep row 2.

Shoulder Shaping
Row 29 [29, 31]: Ch 1, sc in each of first 6 [6, 7] sc, fasten off, sk next 7 [9, 9] sc for neck opening, attach yarn in next sc, ch 1, sc in same sc, sc in each of next 5 [5, 6] sc, fasten off.

Left Front
Row 1: Holding 1 strand each color tog, ch 14 [15, 18], sc in 2nd ch from hook, sc in each rem ch across, turn. *(13 [14, 17] sc)*
Row 2: Ch 1, sc in each sc across, turn.
Rows 3–18: Rep row 2.

Armhole Shaping
Row 19: Sl st in each of first 3 [3, 4] sts, ch 1, sc in same sc as last sl st, sc in each rem sc across, turn. *(11 [12, 14] sc)*
Rows 20–26 [20–26, 20–28]: Rep row 2.

CONTINUED ON PAGE 170

WESTERN SWING PONCHO

You don't have to be a cowgirl to wear this playful poncho dressed up with funky, feathery fringe.

EASY

5 BULKY

Finished Size

18 x 48 inches, excluding
   Fringe

Materials

- Lion Brand Lion Suede bulky (chunky) weight yarn (3 oz/122 yds/85g per skein):
   3 skeins #210-125 mocha
- Size Q/16mm crochet hook or size needed to obtain gauge
- Yarn needle
- Stitch marker

Gauge

7 sts = 4 inches; 6 rows = 4 inches

Pattern Notes

Weave in loose ends as work progresses.
The foundation chain becomes the neck opening and shoulder seam.

Poncho

Row 1: Ch 25 *(this forms the shoulder)*, place a marker

CONTINUED ON PAGE 171

A NIGHT ON THE TOWN

Ideal for all figure types, this sassy little shrug works up in an evening and can be dressed up or down.

EASY

BULKY 5

Finished Size
41 x 44½ inches

Materials
• Moda Dea Bow Ties bulky (chunky) weight yarn (1¾ oz/67 yds/50g per skein): 4 skeins #3737 splash
• Sizes N/15/10mm Q/16mm crochet hook or size needed to obtain gauge
• Yarn needle
• Stitch markers

Gauge
Size Q hook: 4 rows = 4 inches; [1 shell, 1 sc] twice = 4 inches

Pattern Notes
Weave in loose ends as work progresses. Join rounds with a slip stitch unless otherwise stated.

Special Stitches
Shell: 3 dc in indicated st.
Beginning shell (beg shell): Ch 3 *(counts as first dc)*, 2 dc in same st as beg ch-3.

CONTINUED ON PAGE 171

BIG SISTER HOODIE

The tried and true hoodie is made over for a dressier look using color-matched buttons and glittering chunky yarn.

INTERMEDIATE

5
BULKY

Finished Sizes
12 [14, 16]

Finished Garment Measurements
Bust: 32 [34, 36] inches

Materials
- Caron Glimmer chenille bulky (chunky) weight yarn (1¾ oz/49 yds/50g per skein):
    9 [9, 10] skeins each #0009 willow and #0015 iris
- Sizes L/11/8mm and Q/16mm crochet hooks or size needed to obtain gauge
- Tapestry needle
- ¾-inch purple shank buttons: 5 [5, 6]
- Stitch marker

Gauge
Size Q hook: 9 sts = 8 inches

Pattern Notes
Weave in loose ends as work progresses.
Join rounds with a slip stitch unless otherwise stated.

Back
Row 1: With size Q hook and 1 strand each color held tog, ch 20 [22, 24], sc in 3rd ch from hook *(counts as dc and sc)*, [dc in next ch, sc in next ch] across, turn. *(18 [20, 22] sts)*

Row 2: Ch 2 *(counts as first dc)*, sc in dc, [dc in next sc, sc in next dc] across, ending with sc in end ch, turn. Rep row 2 until Back measures 11½ [12, 12½] inches from beg.

Armhole Shaping

Sl st in next st, sc in each dc, dc in each sc across to last st, turn, leaving last st unworked. *(16 [18, 20] sts)* Rep row 2 of Back until armhole measures 8 [8½, 9] inches from beg, fasten off.

Front
Make 2.

Row 1: With size Q hook and 1 strand each color, ch 11 [13, 13], sc in 2nd ch from hook, [dc in next ch, sc in next ch] across, turn. *(10 [12, 12] sts)*

Row 2: Ch 1, sc in each dc, dc in each sc across, turn. Rep row 2 until Front measures 11½ [12, 12½] inches from beg, ending at armhole edge, turn.
Sl st in first st, work in pattern of sc in each dc and dc in each sc across, turn. *(9 [11, 11] sts)*
Continue in pattern until armhole measures 6 [6½, 7] inches, ending at front opening edge, turn.
Sl st in each of next 4 [5, 5] sts, ch 1, working in pattern of sc in each dc and dc in each sc across, work on rem 5 [6, 6] sts until Front measures the same as Back, fasten off.
Sew Back to each Front across shoulder

Sleeve
Make 2.

Row 1: With size Q hook, attach 1 strand each color at underarm, ch 1, work 8 [9, 10] sc sts from underarm to shoulder, work another 8 [9, 10] sc evenly sp from shoulder to underarm. *(16 [18, 20] sc)*

Row 2: Ch 1, [sc in next st, dc in next st] across, turn.

Row 3: Ch 1, work sc in each dc and dc in each sc across, turn. Rep row 3 until Sleeve measures 11 [12, 12½] inches from beg.

Sc dec *(see Stitch Guide)* in next 2 sts, maintaining pattern across row to last 2 sts, sc dec in last 2 sts, turn. *(14 [16, 18] sts)*
Rep row 3 until Sleeve measures 13 [14, 14½] inches

CONTINUED ON PAGE 171

LITTLE SISTER HOODIE

This classic hoodie, stitched in warm shades of cozy bulky yarn, is perfect for a cold day or for one with just the slightest nip in the air.

INTERMEDIATE

5 BULKY

Finished Sizes
Girls size 4 [6, 8]

Finished Garment Measurements
Chest: 26 [28, 30] inches

Materials
- Caron Bliss bulky (chunky) weight yarn (1¾ oz/82 yds/50g per skein):
    5 [5, 6] skeins each #0005 copper and #0006 coral
- Sizes M/13/9mm and Q/16mm crochet hooks or size needed to obtain gauge
- Tapestry needle
- Straight pins

Gauge
Size Q hook: 11 sts = 8 inches

Pattern Notes
Weave in loose ends as work progresses.
Join rounds with a slip stitch unless otherwise stated.

Back
Row 1: With size Q hook and 1 strand of each color held tog, ch 19 [20, 21] sc in 2nd ch from hook, sc in each rem ch across, turn. *(18 [19, 20] sc)*
Row 2: Ch 1 *(counts as first sc)*, sk first sc, sc in each sc across, ending with sc in end ch, turn. *(18 [19, 20] sc)*
Rep row 2 until Back measures 9½ [10, 10½] inches from beg.

Armhole Shaping
Row 1: Sl st in next sc, ch 1, sc in each st across to last st, leaving last st unworked, turn. *(16 [17, 18] sc)*
Rep row 2 until armhole measures 7 [7½, 8] inches, fasten off.

Front
Rep the same as Back until Front above armholes measures 5½ [6, 6½] inches.

Left Neck Shaping
Row 1: Ch 1, sc in each of next 5 sc, turn. *(5, [5, 5] sc)*
Rep row 1 until armhole measures 7 [7½, 8] inches, fasten off.

Right Neck Shaping
Row 1: Sk next 6 [7, 8] sc, attach 1 strand each color in next sc, ch 1, sc in same sc, sc in each rem 4 [4, 4] sc, turn.
Row 2: Ch 1, sc in each of next 5 [5, 5] sc, turn.
Rep row 2 until armhole measures 7 [7½, 8] inches, fasten off.
Holding Front and Back tog, sew shoulder seams.

Sleeve

Make 2.

Row 1 (RS): With size Q hook, attach 1 strand each color at underarm, ch 1, work 8 [8, 9] sc evenly sp to shoulder seam, work 8 [8, 9] sc from shoulder seam to underarm, turn. *(16 [16, 18] sc)*

Row 2: Ch 1, sc in each sc across, turn.

Rep row 2 until Sleeve measures 11 [11½, 12] inches. Change to size M hook, work 2 more sc rows, fasten off.

CONTINUED ON PAGE 172

JUST US GIRLS

Triple the fun and stylish good looks with this trio of vests made with one easy pattern and different yarns.

EASY

Finished Sizes

Girls size 4 [6, 8]

5 BULKY

6 SUPER BULKY

Finished Garment Measurements

Chest: 26 [30, 34] inches

Materials

- Size 4: Lion Brand Homespun bulky (chunky) weight yarn (6 oz/185 yds/170g per skein):
    1 skein #311 rococo
- ¼-inch-wide gold ribbon: 27 yds
- Size 6: Red Heart Light & Lofty super bulky (super chunky) weight yarn (6 oz/140 yds/170g per skein):

- 7 oz/163 yds/193g #9316 puff
- Nobo Boundaries bulky (chunky) weight yarn (1¾ oz/65 yds/50g per skein):
    1 skein #16 Stella
- Size 8: Red Heart Baby Clouds super bulky (super chunky) weight yarn (6 oz/140 yds/170g per skein):
    1 skein #9353 lavender
- Nobo Boundaries bulky (chunky) weight yarn (1¾ oz/65 yds/50g per skein):
    1 skein #1 Christina
- Size Q/16mm crochet hook or size needed to obtain gauge
- Large-eye blunt tapestry needle

Gauge

Size 4: 4 sc = 3 inches; 4 sc rows = 2¾ inches
Sizes 6 & 8: 4 sc = 3¾ inches; 4 sc rows = 3 inches

Pattern Notes

Weave in loose ends as work progresses.

Join rounds with a slip stitch unless otherwise stated.

First Front

Make 2.

Row 1: Starting at bottom edge with 1 strand each color yarn *(or ribbon)* as indicated for each size, ch 7 [8, 8], sc in 2nd ch from hook, sc in each rem ch across, turn. *(6 [7, 7] sc)*

Row 2: Ch 1, sc in each sc across, turn.

Rows 3 & 4 [3 & 4, 4–5]: Rep row 2.

Row 5 [5, 6]: Ch 1, 2 sc in first sc, sc in each rem sc across, turn. *(7 [8, 8] sc)*

Row 6 [6, 7]: Ch 1, sc in each of next 5 [6, 6] sc, leaving rem 2 sc unworked for armhole, turn. *(5 [6, 6] sc)*

Row 7 [7, 8]: Ch 1, **sc dec** *(see Stitch Guide)* in next 2 sts, sc in rem 3 [4, 4] sc, turn. *(4 [5, 5] sc)*

Rows 8 & 9 [8 & 9, 9 & 10]: Rep row 2.

Row 10 (size 4 only): Rep row 2. *(4 sc)*

Row [10, 11] (sizes 6 & 8 only): Rep row [7, 8]. *([4, 4] sc)*

Rows 11 & 12 [11, 12]: Rep row 2.

Row 13 [12, 13]: Sl st in each of first 2 sts, sc in each of next 2 sts, fasten off.

Second Front

Rows 1–4 [1–4, 1–5]: Rep rows 1–4 [1–4, 1–5] of First Front.

Row 5 (5, 6): Ch 1, sc in each sc across to last sc, 2 sc in last sc, turn. *(7 [8, 8] sc)*

Row 6 [6, 7]: Sl st in each of next 2 sts, sc in each of next 5 [6, 6] sc, turn. *(5 [6, 6] sc)*

Rows 7 [7, 8]: Ch 1, sc in each of next 3 [4, 4] sc, sc dec in next 2 sc, turn. *(4 [5, 5] sc)*

Rows 8 & 9 [8 & 9, 9 & 10]: Rep row 2.

Row 10 (size 4 only): Rep row 2. *(4 sc)*

Row [10, 11] (sizes 6 & 8 only): Rep row [7, 8]. *([4, 4] sc)*

Rows 11 & 12 [11, 12]: Rep row 2.

Row 13 [12, 13]: Ch 1, sc in each of next 2 sc, sl st in each of next 2 sc, fasten off.

Back

Row 1: Starting at bottom edge with 1 strand each color yarn *(2 strands rococo for size 4)* as indicated for each size, ch 17 [17, 17], sc in 2nd ch from hook, sc in each rem ch across, turn. *(16 [16, 16] sc)*

Row 2: Ch 1, sc in each sc across, turn.

Rows 3–5: Rep row 2.

Row [6] (size 8 only): Ch 1, 2 sc in first sc, sc in each sc across to last sc, 2 sc in last sc, turn. *([18] sc)*

Row 6 [6, 7]: Sl st in each of next 2 [2, 3] sc, ch 1, sc in same st as last sl st, sc in each st across until 1 [1, 2] sc rem, leaving last 1 [1, 2] sts unworked, turn. *(14 [14, 14] sc)*

Rows 7 [7, 8]: Ch 1, sc dec in next 2 sc, sc in each sc across to last 2 sc, sc dec in last 2 sc, turn. *(12 [12, 12] sc)*

Rows 8 & 9 (8 & 9, 9 & 10): Rep row 2.

Row 10 [10, 11]: Rep row 7 [7, 8]. *(10 [10, 10] sc)*

First Shoulder Shaping

Row 11 [11, 12]: Ch 1, sc in each of next 5 sc, leaving last 5 sts unworked, turn. *(5 [5, 5] sc)*

Row 12 [12, 13]: Ch 1, sc dec in next 2 sc, sc in each of next 3 sc, turn. *(4 [4, 4] sc)*

Row 13 [13, 14]: Sl st in each of first 2 sts, sc in each of next 2 sts, fasten off. *(2 [2, 2] sc)*

Row 11 [11, 12]: Attach yarn in next unworked st of row 10 [10, 11], ch 1, sc in each of next 5 sc, turn. *(5 [5, 5] sc)*

Row 12 [12, 13]: Ch 1, sc in each of next 3 sc, sc dec in next 2 sc, turn. *(3 [3, 3] sc)*

Row 13 [13, 14]: Sc in each of next 2 sc, sl st in each of next 2 sc, fasten off. *(2 [2, 2] sc)*

Assembly

With RS facing, working in **back lp** *(see Stitch Guide)* of each st, sl st Back to Fronts at shoulders. Sl st side seams closed.

Body Trim

Rnd 1 (RS): Attach 2 strands of yarn at side seam, ch 1, sc evenly sp around entire outer edge, working 2 sc in each Front bottom corner, join in beg sc, fasten off.

Armhole Trim

Make 2.

Rnd 1: Attach 2 strands of yarn at underarm, ch 1, sc evenly sp around armhole opening, join in beg sc, fasten off. ✤

BABY BUMPS

Softly colored textured "bumps" will add hours of delight for Baby. Almost as fascinating as a mobile, babies of all ages will enjoy this blanket.

EASY

Finished Size

41 x 44½ inches

Materials

- Red Heart Soft Baby medium (worsted) weight yarn (solid: 7 oz/575 yds/198g; multi: 6 oz/430 yds/170g per skein):

    3 skeins #7959 giggle print

    2 skeins each #7001 white, #7822 sky blue, #7730 bright pink, #7588 lilac and #7624 lime

- Size Q/16mm crochet hook or size needed to obtain gauge
- Large-eye blunt tapestry needle

Gauge

6 sts = 4 inches; 6 rows = 4 inches

CONTINUED ON PAGE 172

SUNSET SCARF

Capture the vivid hues of a brilliant sunset in the beautiful colors of this super-easy scarf stitched in cloud-soft terry chenille yarn.

BEGINNER

Finished Size
4¼ x 65 inches

BULKY

Materials
- Terry Chenille bulky (chunky) weight yarn: 8 oz summer sunset
- Size Q/16mm crochet hook or size needed to obtain gauge

Gauge
5 sc = 4¼ inches

Pattern Note
Weave in loose ends as work progresses.

Scarf
Row 1: Ch 6, sc in 2nd ch from hook, sc in each rem ch across, turn. *(5 sc)*
Row 2: Ch 1, sc in each sc across, turn.
Rep row 2 until yarn is gone ending at end of a completed row, fasten off. ❖

PAINTED STRIPES RUG

Pretty pastel shades add a soft, unexpected dash of color to any room in your home. Double-strand medium weight yarn makes this rug extra cushy under your toes.

EASY

Finished Size

25 x 26 inches

4 MEDIUM

Materials

- Red Heart Super Saver medium (worsted) weight yarn (solid: 7 oz/364 yds/198g; mult: 6 oz/255 yds/141g per skein):
    1 skein each #316 soft white, #363 pale green and #310 monet
- Size Q/16mm crochet hook or size needed to obtain gauge
- Yarn needle

Gauge

(Sc, ch 1, dc) twice = 3½ inches; 3 rows = 3 inches; 4 dc = 3 inches

Pattern Notes

Weave in loose ends as work progresses.

Join rounds with a slip stitch unless otherwise stated.

Work with 3 strands of yarn held together throughout.

Divide soft white and pale green into 3 balls each.

As Rug progresses and color changes, fasten off only the color not being used in the following rows.

Rug

Row 1: Holding 2 strands of pale green and 1 strand of monet tog, ch 38, sc in 2nd ch from hook, sk next

CONTINUED ON PAGE 173

DECADENCE THROW

As much at home in a fabulous loft apartment as it is in a cozy cottage, this plush throw is the perfect way to showcase a variety of luxe fashion yarns in smaller quantities.

BEGINNER

Finished Size

67 inches square

Materials

- Red Heart Super Saver medium (worsted) weight yarn (7 oz/364 yds/198g per skein):
    1 skein each #313 Aran, #360 café, #365 coffee, #312 black and #332 ranch red
- Red Heart Classic medium (worsted) weight yarn (3½ oz/190 yds/99g per skein):
    2 skeins #339 mid brown
- Moda Dea Metro bulky (chunky) weight yarn (1¾ oz/89 yds/50g per skein):
    2 skeins each #9317 vanilla and #9340 chocolate
- Moda Dea Dream medium (worsted) weight yarn (1¾ oz/93 yds/50g per skein):
    3 skeins each #3101 winter white, #3773 raspberry

and #3002 black
    2 skeins #3335 nutmeg
- Moda Dea Eden bulky (chunky) weight yarn (1¾ oz/83 yds/50g per skein):
    1 skein #5330 earth
- Moda Dea Frivolous medium (worsted) weight yarn (1¾ oz/83 yds/50g per skein):
    2 skeins each #9424 silver fox and #9614 bronze goddess
    1 skein each #9912 berry nice and #9611 spun gold
- Red Heart LTD Foxy bulky (chunky) weight yarn (1¾ oz/89 yds/50g per skein):
    3 skeins #9993 pecan
    1 skein each #9117 sandy
- Red Heart LTD Kiss bulky (chunky) weight yarn (1¾ oz/83 yds/50g per skein):
    1 skein #3994 flame
- Size Q/16mm crochet hook or size needed to obtain gauge
- Yarn needle

Gauge

Each square = 13½ inches; 8 sc = 4 inches

Pattern Notes

Weave in loose ends as work progresses.
Work with 2 strands held together throughout.

Color Sequence

Square 1: Vanilla and winter white.
Square 2: Café and pecan.
Square 3: Aran and winter white.
Square 4: Ranch red and flame.
Square 5: Aran and spun gold.
Square 6: "Super Saver" black and "Dream" black.
Square 7: Ranch red and raspberry.
Square 8: Mid brown and earth.
Square 9: Aran and vanilla.
Square 10: Bronze goddess and chocolate.
Square 11: Ranch red and berry nice.
Square 12: "Super Saver" black and silver fox.
Square 13: Bronze goddess and coffee.
Square 14: Coffee and "dream" black
Square 15: Cafe and pecan.
Square 16: Mid brown and sandy.
Square 17: Rep Square 3.
Square 18: Rep Square 7.
Square 19: Café and nutmeg.
Square 20: Rep Square 6.
Square 21: Coffee and chocolate, working only 23

rows for this Square.

Square 22: Coffee and nutmeg.

Square 23: Rep Square 12.

Square 24: Rep Square 15.

Square 25: Rep Square 7.

Square

Make 25.

Row 1: Leave a 15-inch length of yarn at beg, ch 21, sc in 2nd ch from hook, sc in each rem ch across, turn. *(20 sc)*

Rows 2–25: Ch 1, sc in each sc across, turn. At the end of last rep, leaving a 15-inch length of yarn, fasten off.

Square Placement

Sew squares tog with rem beg and ending lengths of yarn.

5	10	15	20	25
4	9	14	19	24
3	8	13	18	23
2	7	12	17	22
1	6	11	16	21

To reduce excess stretching of throw, turn next Square being attached 90 degrees so the last row of that square is joined to the side of the previous Square. ❧

DRAMATIC EFFECTS

Super bulky yarn and rich colors combine for a chunky throw that will keep you warm and add a little drama to your decor!

INTERMEDIATE

SUPER BULKY

Finished Size

46 x 62 inches

Gauge

6 sc = 5 inches; 6 rows = 5 inches

Pattern Notes

Weave in loose ends as work progresses.
Join rounds with a slip stitch unless otherwise stated.
Entire Throw is crocheted with 2 strands held tog throughout.

Special Stitch

Long single crochet (long sc): Insert hook in st 2 rows below, yo, draw up a lp level with working row, yo, draw through 2 lps on hook.

Materials

- Red Heart Light & Lofty super bulky (super chunky) weight yarn (6 oz/140 yds/170g per skein):
    6 skeins each #9312 onyx and #9376 wine
- Size Q/16mm crochet hook or size needed to obtain gauge
- Yarn needle

Throw

Row 1: Holding 2 strands of onyx tog, ch 57, sc in 2nd ch from hook, sc in each rem ch across, turn. *(56 sc)*

Row 2: Ch 1, sc in each sc across, **change color** *(see Stitch Guide)* in last sc to 2 strands of wine, turn.

Row 3: Ch 1, sc in each of next 2 sc, [**long sc** *(see Special Stitch)* in next sc, sc in each of next 2 sc] across, turn. *(18 long sc; 38 sc)*

Row 4: Ch 1, sc in each st across, change color in last sc to 2 strands of onyx, turn.

Row 5: Ch 1, sc in each of next 2 sc, [long sc in next sc, sc in each of next 2 sc] across, turn.

Row 6: Ch 1, sc in each st across, change color in last sc to 2 strands of wine, turn.

Rows 7–54: Rep rows 3–6 consecutively.

Border

Row 1 (WS): Working in side edge of rows, attach 2 strands of onyx, ch 1, sc in end of each row across, turn.

Row 2 (RS): Ch 1, sc in each sc across, fasten off.

Row 3 (WS): Working in side edge of rows on opposite side of throw, attach 2 strands of onyx, ch 1, sc in each row across, turn.

Row 4 (RS): Ch 1, sc in each sc across, fasten off.

Rnd 5 (RS): Attach 2 strands of wine in any sc of row 4, ch 1, sc in each sc around working 3 sc in each corner st, join in beg sc, fasten off. ❧

WATERCOLOR STRIPES PULLOVER CONTINUED FROM PAGE 150

Finishing

Using 1 strand of cotton, with RS of Front and Back facing, measure 5 [5½, 6] inches in from each top end and sew each for shoulder seams. Measure 7 [7½, 8] inches down from shoulder for armhole opening, sew rem for side seam.

Armhole Trim

Rnd 1 (RS): With size L hook, attach 1 strand each color at underarm, ch 1, sc evenly sp around armhole opening, join in beg sc, fasten off.

Bottom Trim

Rnd 1: With size L hook, attach 1 strand each color at side seam, ch 1, sc evenly sp around bottom edge of Pullover, join in beg sc.

Rnd 2: Ch 1, sc in each sc around, join in beg sc, fasten off.

Neckline Trim

Rnd 1: With size L hook, attach 1 strand each color at right shoulder seam, ch 1, sc evenly sp along Back neck, sc evenly sp on left Front working 3 sc in corner st, sc down left Front opening, sc up right Front opening, at top right corner (sc, ch 3, sc) in corner st *(buttonhole lp)*, sc evenly sp to right shoulder, sl st to join in beg sc, fasten off.

Sew button opposite buttonhole lp. ✤

SHADES OF TWILIGHT JACKET CONTINUED FROM PAGE 152

Neck Shaping

Row 27 [27, 29]: Ch 1, sc in each of next 7 [7, 8] sc, turn. *(7 [7, 8] sc)*

Row 28 [28, 30]: Ch 1, **sc dec** *(see Stitch Guide)* in next 2 sc, sc in each rem sc across, turn. *(6 [6, 7] sts)*

Row 29 [29, 31]: Rep row 2, fasten off.

Right Front

Rows 1–18: Rep rows 1–18 of Left Front.

Row 19: Ch 1, sc in each of next 11 [12, 14] sc, turn.

Rows 20–26 [20–26, 20–28]: Rep row 2.

Neck Shaping

Row 27 [27, 29]: Sl st in each of next 5 [6, 7] sts, ch 1, sc in same st as last sl st, sc in each rem sc across, turn. *(7 [7, 8] sc)*

Row 28 [28, 30]: Ch 1, sc in each sc across to last 2 sc, sc dec in next 2 sc, turn. *(6 [6, 7] sc)*

Rows 29 [29, 31]: Rep row 2, fasten off.

Sleeve

Make 2.

Row 1: Holding 1 strand each color tog, ch 16 [16, 19] sc in 2nd ch from hook, sc in each rem ch across, turn. *(15 [15, 18] sc)*

Row 2: Ch 1, sc in each sc across, turn.

Rep row 2, inc 1 sc at each end of 5th [5th, 7th] row and every following 6th row to 21 [21, 24] sc.

Then rep row 2 until 25 [25, 27] rows are completed, fasten off.

Finishing

Use medium weight yarn for sewing seams. Sew Shoulder seams. Sew Sleeve in place having center top of Sleeve at Shoulder seam. Sew Sleeve and side seams.

Neck Edging

Row 1 (RS): Attach 1 strand each color at Right Front corner of neckline, ch 1, sc evenly sp around neckline to Left Front corner, turn.

Row 2: Ch 1, sc in each sc of previous row, fasten off. ✤

WESTERN SWING PONCHO CONTINUED FROM PAGE 154

in the 25th st, ch 35 *(this is the neck opening which now will form a ring)* sc in the ch with the st marker, sc in each of next 24 chs, turn. *(25 sc; ch 35)*

Row 2: Ch 1, working in **front lp** *(see Stitch Guide)* of each sc only, sc in each of next 25 sc, sc in each of next 35 ch sts, working on opposite side of beg ch 25, sc in each of next 25 chs, turn. *(85 sc)*

Row 3: Ch 1, working in front lp of each st, sc in each st across, turn.

Rows 4–27: Rep row 3

Fringe

Cut yarn in 15-inch lengths, [hold 3 strands tog, fold in half, insert hook in end of row, draw strands through at fold to form a lp on hook, draw cut ends through lp on hook, pull gently to secure] across in end of each row. ✤

A NIGHT ON THE TOWN CONTINUED FROM PAGE 155

Shrug

Row 1: With size Q hook, ch 26, sc in 2nd ch from hook, [sk 1 ch, **shell** *(see Special Stitches)* in next ch, sk 1 ch, sc in next ch] across, turn. *(6 shells)*

Row 2: Beg shell *(see Special Stitches)* in first st, [sc in center dc of shell, shell in next sc] across, turn. *(7 shells)*

Row 3: Beg shell in first st, sc in next st, [shell in next sc, sc in center dc of next shell] across, ending with shell in last st of row, turn. *(8 shells)*

Rows 4–18: Rep row 3. *(23 shells)*

With st markers, mark the center 7 shells of row 18. This forms the back neck edge.

Lay the Shrug flat so that the first row is at the bottom and the last row *(with st markers)* is at the top. Top left corner is "A," the bottom left corner is "B," the top right corner is "C" and the bottom right corner is "D." Fold corner A to B and corner C to D.

With length of yarn sew a seam at A/B for 4 inches to form first sleeve seam and then sew a seam at C/D for 4 inches to form 2nd sleeve seam.

Trim

Rnd 1 (RS): With size N hook, attach yarn at bottom center back, ch 1, sc in each st around outer edge until first st marker, [sk 1 st, sc in each of next 2 sts] across to 2nd marker, continue to sc evenly sp around rem outer edge, join in beg sc, remove markers.

Rnd 2: Ch 1, working in **back lp** *(see Stitch Guide)* of each sc, sc in each st around, join in beg sc, fasten off. ✤

BIG SISTER HOODIE CONTINUED FROM PAGE 157

from beg, changing to size L hook rep row 3 until Sleeve measures 15 [16, 16½] inches, fasten off. Sew Sleeve and side seams.

Hood

Row 1: Mark center Back neck with a st marker, starting 2 [2, 2½] inches in from right front edge with RS facing, with size Q hook, attach 1 strand each color, ch 1, work 11 [11, 12] sc sts to st marker, work 11 [11, 12] sc from st marker to within 2 [2, 2½] inches from left front edge, turn. *(22 [22, 24] sc)*

Row 2: Ch 1, [sc in next st, dc in next st] across, turn.

Row 3: Ch 1, sc in each dc and dc in each sc across, turn. Rep row 3 until Hood measures 13½ [14, 14½] inches from beg, fasten off. Fold last row of Hood in half and sew across edge.

Left Front Border

Row 1: With size L hook, attach 2 strands of iris at top left, ch 1, work 26 [27, 28] sc evenly sp to bottom corner, turn.

Row 2: Ch 1, sc in each of next 26 [27, 28] sc, fasten off.

Right Front Border

Row 1: With size L hook, attach 2 strands of iris at bottom right, ch 1, work 26 [27, 28] sc up right edge, turn.

Row 2: Ch 1, sc in first sc, [ch 1, sk 1 sc, sc in each of next 4 sc] 4 [4, 5] times, ch 1, sk 1 sc, sc in each of next 4 [5, 1] sc, turn. *(5 [5, 6] buttonholes)*

Row 3: Ch 1, sc in each sc and each ch-1 sp up Right Front, work 3 sc in corner st, work 3 [3, 4] sc along neck edge, 13 [14, 15] sc to center Hood seam, 13 [14, 15] sc along opposite edge of Hood, 3 [3, 4] sc on neck edge, 3 sc in Left Front corner, sc in each sc down Left Front, fasten off.

Sew buttons opposite buttonholes. ❖

LITTLE SISTER HOODIE CONTINUED FROM PAGE 159

Sew sleeve and side seams.

Pocket

Row 1: With size Q hook and 1 strand each color, ch 17 [18, 19], sc in 2nd ch from hook, sc in each rem ch across, turn. *(16 [17, 18] sc)*

Rows 2 & 3: Ch 1, sc in each sc across, turn.

Row 4: Ch 1, **sc dec** *(see Stitch Guide)* in next 2 sc, sc in each sc across to last 2 sc, sc dec in next 2 sc, turn. *(14 [15, 16] sc)*

Rows 5–7: Rep row 4. *(8 [9, 10] sc)*

Rows 8 & 9: Ch 1, sc in each sc across, turn. At the end of row 9, fasten off.

Center Pocket on Front of pullover and sew bottom edge and rows 1–3 and top edge row 9.

Hood

Row 1: With size Q hook and 1 strand each color, ch 21 [22, 23], sc in 2nd ch from hook, sc in each rem ch across, turn. *(20 [21, 22] sc)*

Row 2: Ch 1, sc in each sc across, turn.

Rep row 2 until Hood measures 11½ [12, 12½] inches, fasten off.

Fold Hood in half, centering row 1 of Hood on Back neck, pin in place, sew in place, fold last row of Hood in half and sew top seam closed.

Tie

With size M hook and 1 strand each color, ch 90 [90, 96], fasten off.

Starting at center front neck edge, weave Tie in and out of edge of Hood, ending back at center front, tie ends in a bow. ❖

BABY BUMPS CONTINUED FROM PAGE 163

Pattern Notes

Weave in loose ends as work progresses.

Join rounds with a slip stitch unless otherwise stated.

Blanket

Row 1 (RS): Holding 1 strand each color tog throughout, ch 60, sc in 2nd ch from hook, sc in each rem ch across, turn. *(59 sc)*

Row 2: Ch 1, sc in first sc, [insert hook in next sc, yo, draw up a lp, ch 3, yo, draw through 2 lps on hook, sc in next sc] 29 times, turn.

Row 3: Ch 1, sc in each st across, turn. *(59 sc)*

Row 4: Ch 1, sc in each of next 2 sc, [insert hook in next sc, yo, draw up a lp, ch 3, yo, draw through 2 lps on hook, sc in next sc] 28 times, sc in last sc, turn.

Row 5: Rep row 3.

Rows 6–65: Rep rows 2–5 consecutively.

Rows 66 & 67: Rep rows 2 and 3. At the end of last rep, fasten off.

Border

Rnd 1 (RS): Holding 1 strand each color tog, attach yarn in corner st, ch 1, [3 sc in corner st, sc evenly sp across edge to next corner] around, join in beg sc.

Rnd 2: [Ch 2, hdc in first ch of ch-2, sk 1 sc, sl st in next sc] around, ending with last sl st in same st as beg ch-2, fasten off. ✿

PAINTED STRIPES RUG CONTINUED FROM PAGE 165

2 chs, [(sc, ch 1, dc) in next ch, sk next 2 chs] 11 times, sc in last ch, turn.

Row 2: Ch 1, sc in first sc, [(sc, ch 1, dc) in next ch-1 sp] 11 times, sc in last sc, turn.

Rows 3–5: Rep row 2.

Row 6: Attach 2 strands of soft white and 1 strand monet in first sc, rep row 2.

Rows 7–10: Rep row 2.

Row 11: Attach 3 strands pale green in first sc, rep row 2.

Rows 12 & 13: Rep row 2.

Row 14: Attach 2 strands of pale green and 1 strand monet in first sc, rep row 2.

Rows 15 & 16: Rep row 2.

Row 17: Attach 3 strands soft white in first sc, rep row 2.

Rows 18 & 19: Rep row 2.

Row 20: Attach 2 strands of soft white and 1 strand monet in first sc, rep row 2.

Rows 21 & 22: Rep row 2. At end of last rep, fasten off turn.

Border

Row 1: Attach 3 strands of soft white in row 22, ch 3 *(counts as first dc)*, [dc in next dc, sk ch-1 sp, dc in next sc] 11 times, 3 dc in last sc, 25 dc evenly sp across ends of rows to next corner, turn. *(51 dc)*

Row 2: Ch 3, dc in each dc to center corner dc, 2 dc in center corner dc, dc in each rem dc across, fasten off.

Row 3: Attach 3 strands of pale green in first dc of row 2, ch 3, 2 dc over side edge of row 2 of Border, 2 dc over side edge of row 1 of Border, work 22 dc evenly sp across opposite side of foundation ch, 3 dc in corner, 22 dc evenly sp across ends of rows, 2 dc in side edge of row 1 of Border, 2 dc in side edge of row 2 of Border, turn.

Row 4: Rep row 2 of Border, fasten off. ✿

GENERAL INSTRUCTIONS

Please review the following information before working the projects in this book. Important details about the abbreviations and symbols used are included.

Hooks

Crochet hooks are sized for different weights of yarn and thread. For thread crochet, you will usually use a steel crochet hook. Steel crochet-hook sizes range from size 00 to 14. The higher the number of the hook, the smaller your stitches will be. For example, a size 1 steel crochet hook will give you much larger stitches than a size 9 steel crochet hook. Keep in mind that the sizes given with the pattern instructions were obtained by working with the size thread or yarn and hook given in the materials list. If you work with a smaller hook, depending on your gauge, your project size will be smaller; if you work with a larger hook, your finished project's size will be larger.

Gauge

Gauge is determined by the tightness or looseness of your stitches, and affects the finished size of your project. If you are concerned about the finished size of the project matching the size given, take time to crochet a small section of the pattern and then check your gauge. For example, if the gauge called for is 10 dc = 1 inch, and your gauge is 12 dc to the inch, you should switch to a larger hook. On the other hand, if your gauge is only 8 dc to the inch, you should switch to a smaller hook.

If the gauge given in the pattern is for an entire motif, work one motif and then check your gauge.

Understanding Symbols

As you work through a pattern, you'll quickly notice several symbols in the instructions. These symbols are used to clarify the pattern for you: brackets [], curlicue braces {}, parentheses () and asterisks *.

Brackets [] are used to set off a group of instructions worked a specific number of times. For example, "[ch 3, sc in next ch-3 sp] 7 times" means to work the instructions inside the [] seven times.

Occasionally, a set of instructions inside a set of brackets needs to be repeated, too. In this case, the text within the brackets to be repeated will be set off with curlicue braces {}. For example, "[dc in each of next 3 sts, ch 1, {shell in next ch-1 sp} 3 times, ch 1] 4 times." In this case, in each of the four times you work the instructions included in the brackets, you will work the section included in the curlicue braces three times.

Parentheses () are used to set off a group of stitches to be worked all in one stitch, space or loop. For example, the parentheses () in this set of instructions, "Sk 3 sc, (3 dc, ch 1, 3 dc) in next st" indicate that after skipping 3 sc, you will work 3 dc, ch 1 and 3 more dc all in the next stitch.

Single asterisks * are also used when a group of instructions is repeated. For example, "*Sc in each of the next 5 sc, 2 sc in next sc, rep from * around, join with a sl st in beg sc" simply means you will work the instructions from the first * around the entire round.

Double asterisks ** are used to indicate when a partial set of repeat instructions are to be worked. For example, "*Ch 3, (sc, ch 3, sc) in next ch-2 sp, ch 3**, shell in next dc, rep from * 3 times, ending last rep at **" means that on the third repeat of the single asterisk instructions, you stop at the double asterisks.

STITCH GUIDE

ABBREVIATIONS

beg	begin/beginning
bpdc	back post double crochet
bpsc	back post single crochet
bptr	back post treble crochet
CC	contrasting color
ch	chain stitch
ch-	refers to chain or space previously made (i.e., ch-1 space)
ch sp	chain space
cl	cluster
cm	centimeter(s)
dc	double crochet
dec	decrease/decreases/decreasing
dtr	double treble crochet
fpdc	front post double crochet
fpsc	front post single crochet
fptr	front post treble crochet
g	gram(s)
hdc	half double crochet
inc	increase/increases/increasing
lp(s)	loop(s)
MC	main color
mm	millimeter(s)
oz	ounce(s)
pc	popcorn
rem	remain/remaining
rep	repeat(s)
rnd(s)	round(s)
RS	right side
sc	single crochet
sk	skip(ped)
sl st	slip stitch
sp(s)	space(s)
st(s)	stitch(es)
tog	together
tr	treble crochet
trtr	triple treble
WS	wrong side
yd(s)	yard(s)
yo	yarn over

Chain—ch: Yo, pull through lp on hook.

Slip stitch—sl st: Insert hook in st, yo, pull through both lps on hook.

Single crochet—sc: Insert hook in st, yo, pull through st, yo, pull through both lps on hook.

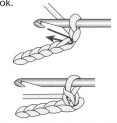

Front loop—front lp Back loop—back lp

Front Loop   Back Loop

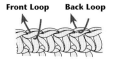

Front post stitch—fp: Back post stitch—bp: When working post st, insert hook from right to left around post st on previous row.

Back   Front

Post of Stitch

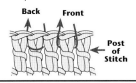

Half double crochet—hdc: Yo, insert hook in st, yo, pull through st, yo, pull through all 3 lps on hook.

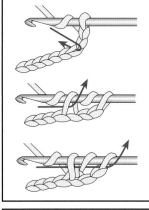

Double crochet—dc: Yo, insert hook in st, yo, pull through st, [yo, pull through 2 lps] twice.

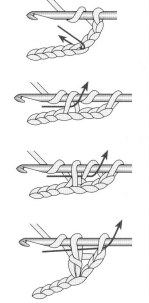

Change colors: Drop first color; with 2nd color, pull through last 2 lps of st.

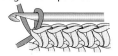

Treble crochet—tr: Yo 2 times, insert hook in st, yo, pull through st, [yo, pull through 2 lps] 3 times.

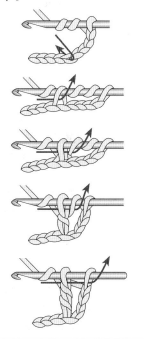

Double treble crochet—dtr: Yo 3 times, insert hook in st, yo, pull through st, [yo, pull through 2 lps] 4 times.

Single crochet decrease (sc dec): (Insert hook, yo, draw up a lp) in each of the sts indicated, yo, draw through all lps on hook.

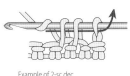

Example of 2-sc dec

Half double crochet decrease (hdc dec): (Yo, insert hook, yo, draw lp through) in each of the sts indicated, yo, draw through all lps on hook.

Example of 2-hdc dec

Double crochet decrease (dc dec): (Yo, insert hook, yo, draw lp through, yo, draw through 2 lps on hook) in each of the sts indicated, yo, draw through all lps on hook.

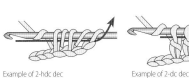

Example of 2-dc dec

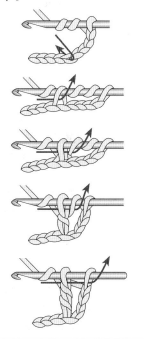

Example of 2-tr dec

Treble crochet decrease (tr dec): Holding back last lp of each st, tr in each of the sts indicated, yo, pull through all lps on hook.

US		UK
sl st (slip stitch)	=	sc (single crochet)
sc (single crochet)	=	dc (double crochet)
hdc (half double crochet)	=	htr (half treble crochet)
dc (double crochet)	=	tr (treble crochet)
tr (treble crochet)	=	dtr (double treble crochet)
dtr (double treble crochet)	=	ttr (triple treble crochet)
skip	=	miss

For more complete information, visit

AnniesAttic.com

SPECIAL THANKS

We would like to acknowledge and thank the following designers whose original work has been published in this collection. We appreciate and value their creativity and dedication to designing quality crochet projects!

Vashti Braha
Mermaid Shrug

Belinda "Bendy" Carter
May Basket

Sue Childress
City Chic Purse

Taryn Christmas
Prima Donna Necklace,
Triple Play

Donna Collinsworth
Bug Rug

JoHanna Dzikowski
Painted Stripes Rug,
Pizzazz on the Prairie

Katherine Eng
Autumn Woods Rug,
Kaleidoscope Colors Cloche

Norma Gale
Neon Stripes Scarf, Twilight
Stripes Rug & Pillow

Cheryl Garcia
Illusion Top, Just Us Girls

Laura Gebhardt
Blue Lagoon, Fireworks
Jacket, Night & Day Jacket,
Ravishing Ruby Pullover,
Shades of Twilight Jacket

Lisa Gonzalez
Honeymoon in Hawaii
Wrap, Tropical Colors Purse

Mary Jane Hall
Leapin' Lizards

Tammy Hildebrand
Beaded Denim Shrug, Blue
Flash Shawl, Dazzling Jade
Jacket, Purple Passion,
Tropical Stripes Bolero,
Vegas Necklace

Margaret Hubert
Big Sister Hoodie, Little
Sister Hoodie, Raggedy
Stripes, Watercolor Stripes
Pullover

Frances Hughes
Midnight Magic Throw,
Scarlet Feathers Pillow

Karen Isak
Lumberjack Throw

Jenny King
A Night on the Town,
Brandywine Capelet, Shortie
Sweater, Decadence Throw,
Western Swing Poncho

Jewdy Lambert
Fancy Foot Warmers,
Flights of Fancy Hat & Scarf,
Hand-paint Medley, Lace
So Simple, Northern Lights
Scarf & Mittens, Something
to Treasure, Sunset Scarf,
Winter Blues

Zena Low
Cool Crochet Cardigan

Joyce Messenger
Fruit Stripes Throw

Christine Grazioso Moody
Cascades, Dramatic Effects,
Midnight Jewels Afghan,
Shades of the Southwest

Freddie Schuh
A Whiz of a Sweater

Darla Sims
Happy Colors Jacket & Hat

Mary Ann Sipes
Aztec Dreams Throw,
Diamonds Are Forever,
Disco Dazzle, Feather Soft
Wrap

Dee Stanziano
Boudoir Elegance Pillow,
Fruit Fantasy Hat

Kathleen Stuart
Edward the Sweater Bear

Aline Suplinskas
Plum Pizzazz Scarf & Hat

Michele Thompson
Baby Bumps, Caliente,
Heartfelt Bag

Margret Willson
Gossamer Throw, Luxurious
Mosaic Throw, Plush
Pullover

Glenda Winkleman
Beverly Hills Glitz, Crayon
Colors Tote, Floral Granny
Afghan, Misty Meadow,
Rustic Retreat Rug

BUYER'S GUIDE

Caron International
P.O. Box 222
Washington, DC 27889
(800) 627-4531
www.caron.com

Coats & Clark
P.O. Box 12229
Greenville, SC 29612-0229
(800) 648-1479
www.coatsandclark.com

DMC Corp.
S. Hackensack Ave.
Port Kearny Building 10F
South Kearny, NJ 07032
(800) 275-4117
www.dmc.com

Lion Brand Yarn Co.
135 Kero Road
Carlstadt, NJ 07072
(800) 258-9276
www.lionbrand.com

N. Y. Yarns
Tahki-Stacy Charles Inc.
70-30 80th Street
Building 36
Ridgewood, NY 11385
(800) 338-YARN
www.nyyarns.com

Plymouth Yarn Company
P.O. Box 28
Bristol, PA 19007
215-788-0459
pyc@plymouthyarn.com

Spinrite
320 Livingstone Ave. S.
Listowel, ON
N4W 3H3 Canada
(800) 265-2864
www.bernat.com